Namo tassa Bhagavato Arahàto Sammasam Buddhassa.

ADORATION TO THE BLESSED, SINLESS, EXALTED ALL KNOWING BUDDHA.

The
Arya Dharma of Sakya Muni, Gautama Buddha.

OR

The Ethics of Self Discipline.

BY THE VENERABLE

THE ANAGARIKA DHARMAPALA,

BRAHMACHARI OF THE BODHISATVA PATH & FOUNDER OF THE MAHA BODHI SOCIETY.

Published by :

MAHA BODHI BOOK AGENCY

*4-A, Bankim Chatterjee Street,
Calcutta-700 073.
INDIA*

First Published 1917

Re-Print 1989

Published by D. L. S. Jayawardana
for Maha Bodhi Book Agency

Printed at PRESS LAND
5A, Bankim Chatterjee Street, Calcutta-73
Phone : 31-6312

TABLE OF CONTENTS.

SECTION I.

SECTION II.

TO

MY SAINTLY MOTHER,

Srimati MALLIKA MAHA UPASIKA.

TO

The Memory of My Beloved Father,

"The Righteous Householder", Well Known For His
Philanthropic Benefactions In Ceylon,

THE MUDALIYAR HEVAVITARANA WIJAYAGUNARATNA ;

TO

MY DEAR "FOSTER MOTHER",

the noble lady

Mrs. T. R. Foster,

of Honolulu, Hawaii To Whose Unfailing Kindness & Munificent
Donations, The Construction of The First Buddhist Vihara
In Calcutta To Enshrine The Sacred Body Relic Of The
LORD BUDDHA, Promised by The Government
Of India To The Maha Bodhi Society,
Has Been Made Possible ;

To the Memory of

Sri NEEL COMUL MOOKERJEE,

Who Lovingly Offered Me Hospitality When I First
Came To Calcutta In March, 1891,

And To Every English-Speaking Person Throughout The World,

This little Volume is Dedicated by

THE

ANAGARIKA BRAHMACHARI DHARMAPALA.

PREFACE

Anagarika Dharmapala, a noble son of Sri Lanka who was the leading light of the Buddhist revival in India in recent times has written several books and pamphlets in addition to editing the oldest Buddhist journal "The Maha Bodhi" the official organ of the Maha Bodhi Society of India from 1892 onwards. The Anagarika Dharmapala founded the Maha Bodhi Society of India in 1891 to safeguard the Buddhagaya temple for the Buddhists of the world and to spread the message of Love and Compassion and the noble Dhamma of the Lord Buddha in India and the world.

To achieve the noble purpose of reviving and spreading the Dhamma in the land of its birth as well as to the western world, he wrote lucidly, with great enthusiasm and an evangelical zeal, many books, foremost of which are the LIFE AND TEACHINGS OF BUDDHA and this book THE ARYA DHARMA OF SAKYA MUNI, GAUTAMA, BUDDHA or THE ETHICS OF SELF DISCIPLINE which was first published in 1917. Through the medium of this book the Anagarika Dharmapala had briefly sketched the life of the Buddha, the great renunciation, a brief comparison of the tenets of Buddhism and the other religions of the world, the exhortation of the Buddha to Kings and to the common laymen on the ethics of day to day family life and a happy home. He has also touched on the psychological aspects of Buddhism, on evolution and creation, on Karma and the fruits of Karma and also given the ancient version of the story of the Genesis as known to the primitive Aryans of India. He has also dealt with Dhyanayoga, the attitudes of the West and some of the eastern countries to Buddhism and also dealt at length on the value of the Pali language for study of Buddhism and also as a unifying media, on the need for the development of art, industry and culture for the economic upliftment and well being of the down-trodden masses of India. On Buddhagaya the holiest of shrines of the Buddhists, the heart of the Anagarika Dharmapala has grieved. He speaks of the role to be played by the Maha Bodhi Society in the upliftment of the quality of life of the common people and the spread of the noble Dhamma to the people of India and the world. The fundamental doctrines of the Buddha Dhamma are clearly and with simplicity presented before the reader in the latter stages of the book and this will prove most helpful to all those who are interested in the study of Buddhism.

As we are entering the 125th Birth Anniversary of the Ven. Anagarika Dharmapala and we are also on the threshold of the Centenary of the founding of the Maha Bodhi Society of India, to pay our deep respects and gratitude to this noble son of Lanka who made India his home and dedicated his entire life for the spread of Buddhism in India and the western countries, we are taking steps to popularies the writings of the Anagarika Dharmapala.

We take this opportunity to express our deep appreciation for the re-print of this valuable and enlightening booklet THE ARYA DHARMA OF SAKYA MUNI, GAUTAMA BUDDHA or THE ETHICS OF SELF DISCIPLINE by the Maha Bodhi Book Agency and we are particularly thankful to Mr. D. L. S. Jayawardena of the Maha Bodhi Book Agency for his enthusiastic effort in getting out this book during this period when the need for the message of Love and Compassion of the Buddha in the world which is full of turmoil, hatred and destructive wars, is felt necessary more than ever before. We congratulate him for taking a keen interest to re-print this book and may the efforts made by publishing this book of spreading the Dhamma be objectively achieved for the welfare of the many and the good of the many. We are thankful to the printers for their excellent work.

May the Message of the Buddha pervade throughout the world.

May all beings be happy !
Sabbe Satta Bhavantu Sukhitatta !

Ven. M. Wipulasara Maha Thera
General Secretary
Maha Bodhi Society of India

4/A, Bankim Chatterjee Street,
Calcutta-700073
2nd January, 1989.

THE ARYA DHARMA OF GAUTAMA, THE BUDDHA.

Hindu under a Rishab. (See Vishnu Purana,
(?Adiwsa. The Buddha religion of the Jains was
founded by Mahavira Vira). The modern
Vedanta philosophy religion is a product of

The
Arya Dharma of Sakya Muni, Gautama, The Buddha.

BUDDHAGAMA AND THE RELIGIONS OF THE WORLD

Europe received its religion from the Asiatic Jews. Peter was a Galilean fisherman, and Paul was a tent-maker of Tarsus. The founder of the religion was Jesus, son of a Jewish Carpenter of Nazareth. Islam was founded by Mahammad, who was by profession a supervisor of a caravan in service under an Arabian lady of Mecca. The religion of Zendavesta was founded by Zoroaster, a Persian. The religion of Jehovah was founded by Moses, a Hebrew born in Egypt. Protestant Christianity was founded by Luther, a German. Vedic Brahmanism was the joint product of Brahman Rishis. The secret religoin of the Upanishads was founded by the Rajarishis of ancient India. Even Yajnāvalkya was

A   1

trained under a Rājarshi. (See Vishnu Purana, 4 Adhyāya.) The Tirthaka religion of the Jains was founded by Mahavira of Vesāli. The modern Vedantism was founded by Sankara, a Brahman of Malabar. Vasishta Advaita religion was founded by the Brahman Rāmānujāchariya, the Dwaita religion was founded by the Brahman Madhvācharya. Vaishnava religion was founded by the Brahman Chaitanya. The religion of the Sikhs was founded by Guru Nanak. The religion of Tao was founded by the Chinese philosopher, Laotsze ; Confucianism was founded by Confucius of China. The modern Brahma Samaj was founded by the Brahman, Rāja Ram Mohan Rai. All these religions have one common basis, except the system of political ethics taught by Confucius. Confucius did not wish to enter into the speculations of the hereafter. His was purely a moral and political system upholding the Conservative government of ancient China. The religion of Tao did not concern with the affairs os this world. The Chinese philosopher was wholly interested in the discovery of the divine principle of Tao, Vedanta, of the Advaita. Vedanta of the Vishistadvaita, and the Vedanta of the Dwaita, the religion of the Vaishnavas of Bengal founded by Chaitanya are of Indian origin, and are post-

Buddhistic. The religion of the Sikhs, the Visishtadvaitism, Dwaitism, Vaishnavism were founded after the invasion of India by the Moslems. The Brahma Samaj was founded after the British occupation of Bengal.

The one religion that stands by itself is the religion promulgated by the Prince of Kapilavastu, Sakya Muni, the Buddha Gotama. Historically it is the oldest religion in the world. Brahmanism underwent modifications after the invasion of India by the Moslems. The religion of Jesus after it was established in European soil was no more the religion of the poor. It became the religion of the diplomatic politician and the dogmatic ecclesiastic.

Islam was first the religion of the political refugees of Mecca, and after the acquisition of political power by Mahammad. it became the religion of Fatalism, and as long as the power of the sword was in the hands of the Moslems it did not cease its conquest. Mahammad did not teach anything new to the people of Mecca, except that he isolated Allah destroying other gods worshipped by the Meccans. The story of Adam and several other stories from the Old Testament of the Bible he borrowed, and gave the creation account as it appeared in the Bible. changing the name of the Creator Jehovah into Allah.

The old customs of circumcision and the worship of the Kaaba, the black stone at Mecca, were adhered to. The ancient temple of Mecca, wherein the Kaaba was, belonged to the family of Mahammad. The very name Mahammad was older than his religion. He kept the old name, even after he became a Conqueror.

Judaism is a mixture of old Babylonian and Egyptian ethics. Judaism and Jehovah are interdependent. I am a holy God thou art a holy people unto me O Israel : that was the cry of the Jehovistic prophets. Judaism lost its place after the Jews returned from their exile in Babylon. The Jews do not care to make converts. So are the Parsees of Bombay. Their religion is only for the Parsees. The Brahmins do not want converts from other castes and countries. Their religious books are in the Sanskrit language, and the non-Brahmans are prohibited from reading the Vedas. The non-Brahman Sudras are religiously under the domination of the Brahmans. No non-Brahman is initiated by the Brahmans, and there is no propaganda of Brahmanism in other lands.

Muhammad from the beginning of his career adopted the military method of the conqueror. The fighting soldier who dies in the battle-field was assured a heaven after death. The martial spirit could not be

4

kept except by good food, and intoxicating drinks
were prohibited since it interferes with the fighting
spirit. This is an old doctrine.

The ancient Kshatriyas of India promised a
heaven to the man who dies fighting in the battle-field.
Sree Krishna in his Bhagavat Gita assured the fighting
man that heaven is his reward. In the Jātaka story
called the Maha Bodhi Jātaka this fact is mentioned.
In the Gamini Samyutta of the Samyutta Nikāya, at
the time of the Buddha this doctrine was prevalent,
that the soldier who dies fighting is born in heaven.
The soldiers were prevented from joining the Bhikkhu
Order as their services were required in the battle-field
by the King. The religion of the Jews was a purely
fighting religion with Jehovah as the commander-in-
Chief of the Judaic forces. All the wars were carried
on by the people of Judah under the command of
Jehovah. All the tactics of the military dictator were
adopted by Jehovah. When he could not manage
the Jews He went and joined the Babylonian king
Nebuchadnezzar, and betrayed the poor Jews to be
taken captives to Babylon. In the Old Testament the
prophets were guided by Jehovah ; in the Koran
Mahammad advised Allah the course to follow.
Whatever Mahammad desired to have was in this way
obtained, inasmuch as Allah was always ready to

comply with the wishes of Mahammad. Jehovah failed in his policy, and he had to abandon the holy mount of Moriah at Jerusalem, although he had made every effort to guide the Jews to victory. The last book of the Old Testament is Malachi, and then there is a long interval without any history of the activities of Jehovah. Again Jehovah appears with the appearance of the prophet of Nazareth. But in a different role. He is the Father of all. For nearly 300 years, the history of Jehovah was a blank, before the advent of Jesus.

Greece, Egypt, Syria, Babylon, Persia, and the country of Gandahar whose capital was Taxila in the time of Asoka came to know of the kingdom of the Gangetic Valley. Long before Alexander came to Gandahar, Taxila was known to the people of the Gangetic valley as a place of learning. From the time of Alexander to the time of the Muhammedan invasion of India there was an overland route from India to Egypt through the Mesopotamian countries. There was communication between China and Egypt through Turkestan. After the invasion of the countries to the west of India by the cohorts of Islam the overland route to India suffered, and gradually forgotten.

The religions of the world may be divided into two categories : Destructive and non-Destructive.

6

Blood sacrificing religions are Vedic Brahmanism, Zorastrianism, Muhammedanism, Judaism, Christianity, Confucianism and Saiva Vedantism ; the non-Destructive religions are Buddhāgama, Jainism and Vaishnava religion of Chaitanya. Jainism adopted the doctrine of ahimsā, but narrowed its usefulness by extreme methods. The religion of the Buddha was a purely psychological science which was taught only to those who were admitted into the Brahmachariya Order of Yellow robed Bhikkhus. The popular religion of gods, hells, pretas, Brahmas, of ancient India without the blood sacrifices, slightly modified was preached by the Buddha to the householders. The householders who followed the Buddha wore white robes. Tirthaka was the name given to the religion of the Jains. In the Buddha's time there were many schools of philosophy, each one showing a way to heaven. The actors, ascetics, soldiers &c. had their own heavens. The Brahmans taught that heaven can be obtained by bathing in the sacred waters of the Ganges and other rivers, and also by means of prayer that souls can be sent to heaven. The chief God of the manvantara whom the people of India accepted was Brahma. He was a God of Love and Compassion. The Buddha was requested by Brahma to save the world. The Brahma qualities

7

of love, compassion, joyousness, contentment were required to be practised to be born in the Brahmaloka. The God of Love paid homage to the Lord Buddha for the supremeness of the Wisdom that the Lord possessed. The Buddha after He had attained the anuttara sambodhi knowledge looked throughout the Universe to whom He should pay homage, and among living gods and Brahmas and Brahmans there was none fit to receive His worship or homage. It was at this moment that the Brahmā appeared before the Lord and said that there is none worthy to receive the homage of a perfect Buddha, and that the Buddha may pay homage to supreme Truth (DHAMMA).

All religions posit a god under different names. He is called Brahmā, Brahman, Isvara, Vishnu, Mahadeva, Siva, Jehovah, Allah, Tao, Elohim, I-am-that-I-am, Jah, Baal, Osiris, Ahuramazda, Ra, Marduk, Kurumasaba, God, Gott, Bhog, Om, &c. The creators of these gods were human beings. Each nation had its own god. The god of Israel was fighting with the gods of Canaan, and he was jealous, and ordered the children of Israel to worship him and no other. Of course they did not listen to him, and he was very angry, because they "went whoring after other gods." In the fight sometimes he is defeated by the god of Babylon, and once the Israelites being

8

defeated by the Philistines, the former fled leaving the tabernacle of god on the field. The god was locked up in the tabernacle, and the Philistines set the tabernacle in a bullock cart, and sent it to the Israelites, and when it was brought to the field and left there, some of the Israelites looked into the tabernacle, with the result God got angry and destroyed several thousands. Jehovah failed to kill the gods which gave him trouble. Mahammad destroyed all the gods of Mecca and kept only one, and isolated him. The Christians say that God created man about 6000 years ago from the earth of Mesapotamia. The God Allah created man about 7000 years ago. The Brahmans say that Brahmā created the four castes, and that they came from his mouth, The Kshatriyas declared that they came from the Sun, and that they are the kinsmen of the Sun. The Vaishyas and Sudras were not interested in philosophical matters, and they were not able to discover a god to represent them. The Kayastas created their own god and called him Chitragupta. The craftsmen created their own god, and they called him Visvakarma. The Russians called their god Bhog. The ancient Romans had Jupiter as their god. The Greeks had Zeus. The ancient Brahmans created innumerable gods to suit the taste of the people. In all they have

9

330 millions gods, and the more the better, and each one had his own Ishtadevata, or his own god who is protecting him, something like the daemon of Socrates. Jesus called his god Our Father. The gods of exoteric religions did not know that the world was many millions years old. Neither the prophets who proclaimed the gods had any idea of the modern sciences of geology, astronomy, paleontology &c. Before the discovery of the sciences of astronomy, geology, and of the element radium, the scientists had no evidence to demonstrate the age of the earth. The antiquities of Egypt, and Babylonia show that there existed civilized races in these countries eight thousand years ago.

The religion of Jews is a mixture of ancient Babylonian and Egyptian myths. Jesus appeared at a time when the Greeks, Romans, Syrians, Persians, Egyptians, Babylonians were still enjoying the fruits of their own civilizations. The ancient Romans did not destroy the ancient religions of Egypt and Assyria &c. The first iconoclasts were the converts to Christianity after the conversion of the Roman emperor Constantine. Then commenced the destruction of the ancient religions, and their temples were all destroyed, and their philosophers burnt. About five hundred years later Mahammad began to preach

10

the religion of Islam, and the victorious Moslems carried fire and sword through countries where the Christians held sway, and Christianity was driven out from Asia Minor and Egpyt. When a nation gains victory in the battle field, the god of the Victorious party is elevated, the defeated god is driven out of the field. So do the gods appear and disappear. Jehovah disappeared and the God our Father came into existence. Ahuramazda was in Persia, but after Persia went under Islam, Ahuramazda was driven out, and Allah took his place.

In the Puranas are given discussions on different subjects, where in the gods and the Rishis took part. In these accounts the gods and Philosophers are engaged in mutual conversation and no jealousy is shown. Mahadeva, Isvara, Shiva, Vishnu, Sri Krishna, Brahma, together with the goddesses are found engaged in conversation with the Rishis. That the world is 7000 years old and that man was created by a god from clay, no philosophic thinker now believes. The creation stories are the myths of childhood of pagan peoples.

The charge of atheism is brought against the religion of the Lord Buddha. Buddha came to teach a path without the help of gods or devils. But the people who had their gods got angry because the Lord

did not want their help. It is like the man who
believed that light can only be got through the burning
of oil and wick. He would not accept any other light
except the oil light, and when the electrician came
and said that he could give a brilliant light without
having recourse to either oil or wick, the oil lamp man
said, that can't be, let me have the electric light with
the oil and the wick put in, and I shall be satisfied.
The muddle-headed who have no idea of the science
of evolution or the science of electricity would not
believe that a brilliant light could be got without the
aid of oil and wick. Buddhism is a religion that
teaches new things which the old god believers had no
conception of. The Lord taught that man can get his
salvation without the help of angry, blood thirsty
deities. The religion that the Lord gave to the
civilized Aryans of ancient India was psychological.
No god is needed to get rid of anger, jealousy, ill-will,
pride, ignorance. It is a religion of internal development, and the angry gods can't help another to get
rid of anger while they themselves were still
dominated by jealousy and anger. Just as light is
obtained by means of the electric dynamo without the
help of oil, wick and match, so man by following the
path of the Lord Buddha, which is the path of
scientific wisdom, can attain the highest peace, bliss

and freedom by individual effort and personal purity of heart.

The Buddhist can admit into the circle of gods Allah, Jehovah, God, Gott, or any other god who may come into existence in the twentieth century. No Buddhist can hate gods. They have to practise the mettābhāvana, and give their love to all the gods. devils, and demons and all living beings. He admits all gods and he gives his love to all. But gods who murder, and get angry, set fire to cities, kill innocent men, women and children, send tornadoes, typhoons, cyclones, earthquakes, thunderstorms, plagues, pestilences, and create the blind, deaf, dumb, the epileptic, the feeble-minded, and the crippled, the Buddhist rejects. Some gods get angry daily, some gods want wine bread and meat for their foods. Some gods without the blood of cows are not happy. Some gods get the worship of muddle-headed by giving them the liberty to kill animals and eat their flesh. They are satisfied with a little music and a few candles and a few psalms. Each man according to his intelligence makes his own god. The Buddhist loves them all and they are given the merits of the good deeds that he does. No god need be angry with a Buddhist.

THE LIFE OF THE BUDDHA, GAUTAMA SAKYA MUNI

Four asankheyya and a hundred thousand kalpas ago there appeared the fully enlightened, omniscient, all compassionate Buddha who was called Dipankara.

At that time there lived Sumedha, a holy Brahman saint, who, when he was a young man became the inheritor of vast wealth of his forefathers. He then began to reflect that this vast wealth, hoarded up from generation to generation, had been left behind by his ancestors for seven generations ; and as they had not made use of it for good, let me use it for the good of the world. Thinking thus he advised his attendants to make it known that the accumulated wealth in the house of the Brahman Sumedha is to be given away in charity. For seven days the vast wealth was given to the poor and the needy, and the seventh day he renounced the pleasures of the world, and went to the Himalayas to practise the rules of sainthood. He attained proficiency in the five abhigñas and the eight samāpatti, and was able to go through the sky to the heavens of the gods.

At this time on a certain day the Brahman Sumedha came down from the Himalayas to the city called Amaravati and he found that the people were busy in decorating the streets and their houses, and he inquired from the people on whose account they are decorating the city for, and they told him that the Holy One, the Buddha Dipankara is expected in their city, and these decorations are in His name. The very hearing of the word Buddha made him glad, and a thrill of joy went through his whole body. He thought that he should also show his reverence to the Buddha by decorating a portion of the road, and he asked them to let him also decorate a portion, and they gave him a portion of the road. The holy Brahman could have easily by his spiritual powers decorated the road, but he by his own hands began decorating the road. Before he could finish his portion, the Buddha was seen coming with the band of holy Arhats in yellow robes. The holy Brahman then resolved to offer his body to the Buddha, and he lay down with his face down wards. and stretched himself, lengthwise for the Buddha to walk over his body. The Buddha approached the holy man, and seeing him, stopped, and beckoning to the Arhats, said, "this holy man, if he so wishes may now pass on to Nirvana by becoming an Arhat, but he wills to be a Buddha like me, and I prophesy that under the name of Gotama, four asankheyyas and a hundred thousand kalpas hence, he will be born in the Sakya family, his father will be the Rājā Suddhodana, and his mother the Queen Māyā, and that he will save countless millions of human and divine beings from the sorrows of Sansāra.

Saying thus, the Buddha Dipamkara, taking a handful of flowers offered to the future Buddha, and the people all rejoiced, and shouted that they will be born when Sumedha becomes Buddha, and get salvation through Him.

The holy Sumedha at that time resolved to fulfil the ten paramitas, which are

> Dāna, Sila, Nekkhamma, Paññā, Viriya, Satya,
> Kshanti, Adhisthāna, Maitri, Upekshā.

Dāna is charity absolute, giving life, wealth, blood, flesh, eyes, children, wife.

Sila is perfection in moral conduct, never deviating from the path of virtue.

Nekkhamma is renunciation of sensual pleasure, and aspiring to lead the saintly life of mercy and holiness.

Paññā is perfect Wisdom to comprehend all the laws of nature which is beyond the grasp of the ordinary man. It is the wisdom of Nirvāna transcending the wisdom of gods and men.

16

Viriya is unceasing, continuous exertion, persevering till death.

Kshānti is forgiving patience. Even when the body is being cut to pieces an angry word must not escape his lips. Only the thought of love should prevail.

Satya is truthfulness even unto death. Never to speak a lie even at the pain of death. Truthfulness is a weapon to defeat the liar.

Adhishtāna is cultivating will power to do the highest act of good. No obstacle makes him despair, and with undaunted will he continues till the consummation is reached.

Maitri is all pervading love to every living creature. It is the love of the mother to the invisible child in the womb.

Upekshā is perfect equanimity, showing the same good feeling to all alike, whether friend or foe.

From the moment that the Buddha prophesied that Sumedha would become a sammā-sam-Buddha, he is a Buddha elect, and hence forward only known as the Bodhisatva Mahasatva. He is greater than all other beings, and his wishes become fulfilled. He may be born as an animal, or god, or Brahmā, but the golden thread runs through life after life, which continues unbroken. For four asankheyya and a hundred

B   17

kalpas he had to go through the path of perfection.
Life after life he has to fulfil the pāramitas. In some
life he may fulfil the paramitā of charity, in another
life another pāramitā, and there is no deviating from
the path. He has become incapable of doing evil.
Under the Buddha Dipamkara he could have reached
Nirvāna, but the Arhatship that was in his possession
he surrendered so that he may become the Buddha,
and save the world. He has no more sin, and now he
is only accumulating merits for the sake of the world,
for their good. He does everything good for the welfare of the world. There is no more egoism in him.
He does his duty and patiently waits. He knows that
he is the future Buddha. He gets the intuitive
knowledge of the Bodhisatva and the fulfilment of the
paramitās becomes easy. He does every act of
sacrifice with delight. Because he knows that at some
future time that he will save the world. He is the
supreme one in every life.

The fulfilment of paramitās is necessary to reach
Nirvāna. The three paths to reach Nirvāna are that of
the Arhat, Pacceka Buddha and Sammāsambuddha.
It is different from the path leading to the heavens of
Brahmas and devas. To reach Nirvāna as an Arhat
the ten pāramitas have to be practised for one
assankheyya kalpa ; to reach Nirvāna as a Pratyeka

18

Buddha, one has to practise the ten pāramītas for two asankheyya kalpas ; and to reach Nirvāna as a sammās-ambuddha there are three ways, by strenuousness, by faith and by wisdom. The Bodhisat who takes the strenuous life are called viriyādhika ; the one who takes the path of faith is called saddhādhika, and the one who takes the path of wisdom is called Paññādhika. The paññādhika Bodhisat has to fulfil the pāramitās for sixteen asankheyya kalpas ; the saddhādhika Bodhisat takes eight asankheyya kalpas and the Viriyadhika Bodhisat takes four assankheyyas and one hundred thousand kalpas. Our Buddha belonged to the viriyadhika class.

The Bodhisatva first received the initiation from the Buddha Dipamkara and then from the Buddhas Kondañña, Tanhamkara, Medamkara, Mangala, Sumana, Revata, Sobhita,. Anomadassi, Paduma, Nārada, Padumuttara, Sumedha, Sujāta, Piyadassi, Atthadassi, Dhammadassi, Siddhattha, Tissa, Phussa, Vipassi, Sikhi, Vessabhu, Kakusandha, Konāgamana and Kassapa.

In the fulfilment of the pāramitas the perfection in each has to be reached by the Bodhisats. The Bodhisat has to say

(*Dāna.*)

1. "In alms there is none can equal me
   In alms have I perfection reached

19

(*Sila.*)

2. They pierced me through with pointed stakes
   They hacked me with their hunting knives
   Yet I was not angry but kept the precepts perfectly

(*Nekkhamma.*)

3. A kingdom dropped into my hands
   Like spittle vile I let it fall
   Nor for it felt the smaller wish
   And thus renunciation gained

(*Pragñā.*)

4. With wisdom sifted I the case
   And freed the Brahman from his woe
   In wisdom none can equal me
   In wisdom I've perfection reached

(*Viriya.*)

5. Far out of sight of land were we
   The crew were all as dead of fright ;
   Yet still unruffled was my mind :
   In courage I've perfection reached.

(*Kshānti.*)

6. Like one insensible I lay,
   While with his hatchet keen he hacked,
   Nor raged against Benares King :
   In patience I've perfection reached.

(*Satya.*)

7. I kept the promise I had made
   And gave my life in sacrifice
   A hundred warriors set I free
   In truth have I perfection reached

(*Adhitthāna.*)

8. "Tis not that I my parents hate
   "Tis not that glory that I detest
   But since omniscience I held dear
   Therefore I kept my firm resolve

(*Maitri.*)

9. No fear has any one of me
   Nor have I fear of any one
   In my good will to all I trust
   And love to dwell in lonely woods

(*Upeksha.*)

10. While from the villages around
    Some came to mock and some to praise
    Indifferent to pain and pleasure
    I acquired the perfection of indifference."

—*Warren.*

In the last birth as Vessantara Prince the perfection
of charity was reached when he gave his two children
to the Brahman as an offering, and his wife, the prin-

21

cess Madri to the god Indra, and after death he was
born in the Tusita heaven, and when the time came
for him to take birth on earth to become Buddha, the
gods approached the future Buddha and solicited Him
to take birth in India for the salvation of the world.
Then the Bodhisat looked to the five great signs of
fulfilment : time, continent, country, mother, family ;
and he found that the time was appropriate, that the
best of the continents was Jambu dipa, the best of
countries was the Middle country of India, and the
best of families was the family of the Sakyas descended
from the Solar King, Ikshvāku, and the best of women
was the Queen Maha Māyā of immaculate conduct.

Ten thousand worlds rejoiced when the future
Buddha left the Tusita devaloka to be conceived in
the immaculate womb of the queen Mahā Māyā. Ten
months after, the time came for delivery and the Queen
went in procession to her own kingdom of Devadāha
and when approaching the royal garden Lumbini, she
felt a desire to visit the garden, and with all the
retinue she entered the garden and was walking under
the shady grove, when the pain of delivery came, and
under the Sāla Tree, the future Buddha was born.

Then came four Gods of the Suddhāvāsa heaven
of immaculate minds, and received the future Buddha,
and placed Him before his mother and said, Rejoice

22

O Queen, a mighty son has been born to you. The four guardian angels then took the child and handed Him to the men, and then at that moment He uttered the words "I am the Chief, the Eldest, in all the world". At the same time the future Buddha was born there were born the future wife Yasodharā, to be known as the mother of Rāhula ; the horse Kanthaka, the courtier Kaludāyi, the charioteer Channa, and the Bodhi Tree at Buddhagaya. The gods of ten thousand worlds rejoiced on the day that the future Buddha was born. (The details of the birth story is given in the Jātaka book, translated by C. H. Warren in his "Buddhism in Translations".)

In the sixteenth year the Prince Siddhartha was married to the princess Yasodharā, and they lived in all happiness till their twenty-ninth year, when the Princess gave birth to a male child, and on that night the Prince Siddhartha made the great renunciation to seek the way of salvation.

On the seventh day of the birth of the future Buddha his mother died and was born in the Tusita heaven, and the divine Child was nursed by the second wife of Rājā Suddhodhana, the Princess Maha Prajā-pati, sister of the late Queen. The Rājā Suddhodana built for the use of the Prince three palaces one for the summer, one for the rainy season and one for the cold weather, and made them like habitations of gods. The Anguttara Nikāya commentary has given details of the three palaces.

After making the great renunciation the Prince Bodhisatva put on the yellow robe and walked on foot from the border of the Sakyan country to the capital of Magadha. He begged his food from the people and went alone to the rock cave on the Pāndava hill and ate his food. Here the Bodhisat was visited by King Bimbisāra, and the young king requested the Bodhisat to stay with him and rule half the kingdom. The Prince Bodhisat told the king that he belongs to the Aditya race, and that he is a Kosala Sakya Prince ; that he left the pleasures of the palace to seek Truth.

Leaving Rajagriha the Bodhisat wandered alone to seek the Brahman rishis and for some time He lived under the two great rishis Alārakālāma and Udraka Rāmaputra, from whom He learnt the philosopyy of the Arupa Brahmaloka. Not satisfied with the results of dhyāna yoga leading to nevasññānāsaññā, the Bodhisat came to Uruvela to spend the ascetic life, and for six years He mortified the body in the hope of reaching the highest bliss. His body by strict fasting was reduced to a mere skeleton, and one day he fell down unconscious, and his friends thought he was

24

dead, and the gods said that he will not die till truth is
found. At last He woke up from the swoon, and then
he abandoned the path of asceticism.

He looked back to find out at what period of life
he was happy when he was in his father's palace, and
the picture of the ploughing scene at Kapilavastu
when he was an infant, sitting alone under the Jambu
tree came before His mind's eye. The idea of
following the middle path came to him, and he found
that the baby life requires everything in moderation.
The phychology of the infant life helped the Bodhisat
to discover the middle path as the road fit for the
Brahmachāri who was in search of Nirvāna. This life
He adopted, and when He began to take food after
the long fasts, the five Brahman companions left the
Bodhisat, and then He was alone.

He began to take food during the middle of the
day, and by slow degrees He recovered the lost flesh,
and on the day of the full moon of the month of
Vesākha (April-May) He went and sat at the foot of
the Ajapala Banyan tree, when He received the milk
food at the hands of Sujātā. In the evening He came
and sat at the foot of the Bodhi Tree resolved never
to get up from the place till the Wisdom of Nirvāna is
realized.

At the first watch of the night He gained the

divine knowledge to look to the past for countless
millions of years, and in the middle watch of the night
He received the divine insight to look to the future,
whereby He was able to see what happens to life at
death. He found that man dies and is born again,
and that according to his deeds he suffers or enjoys.
In the early dawn the great Light of Omniscience He
realized and the working of the great Law of Cause
and Effect was revealed, and He became the
Sammāsam Buddha.

For seven weeks He spent, a week at each place
near about the Bodhi Tree in the enjoyment of the
happiness of final emancipation. No more was He
in samsara, He had become an Arhat. He discovered
the happiness of Eternal Nirvana. No more birth,
and no more death. Sufferings have ceased abso-
lutely. Only Love and Wisdom remain.

Māra the chief god of the heavens came to the
Blessed One and said that now the Tathāgata has
gained final liberation, that He should live in silence,
alone and enjoy rest. The Blessed One answered and
said, Friend of Death, I shall not seek the repose of
Nirvāna in peace and solitude, but I will train men and
women in the discipline and make them Bhikkhus and
Bhikkhunis, and will teach laymen and laywomen
in the Doctrine, and make them to propagate the

sweet Doctrine, and subdue the false doctrines, and then will I seek the final repose.

The Blessed One was requested by the Brahmā Sahampati to preach the Doctrine, and purify the forgotten faith that leadeth to Nirvāna. The Buddha accepted the offer, and began the life of activity to save the world from sin and sorrow by love and wisdom.

From Buddhagaya the Blessed One walked to Benares in search of the five Brahman companions who were His friends at Uruvela. He found them at the Dear Park at Migadava, now Sarnath.

He preached the Doctrine of the Middle path, and the Four Noble Truths, and enunciated the Doctrine of No-Ego-Anatman.

After three months, in the month of October the Blessed One had sixty Bhikkhus, all emancipated from sin and sorrow. They were given the order to proclaim the Doctrine, sweet in the beginning, sweet in the middle, sweet in the end, for the welfare of the many, for their happiness, for their good, with compassion. The sixty Arhats went in sixty directions, and the Blessed One came to Gaya and Uruvela.

At Uruvela He converted the fireworshipping ascetics, chief of whom was Uruvela Kassapa with 500 disciples. Then at Gayāsirsa He converted the two other chief Jatilas, and at the site of Gaya sirsa He preached the Flame sermon to the thousand converted ascetics and they all became Arhats. With the thousand The Blessed One went to Rajagriha to meet the King, Bimbisāra. The King and his court were converted to the new faith. Thence forward for forty five years He went all over India preaching the Dhamma to king, and prince, noble and low, to man and woman, rich and poor, to the beggar and leper without distinction of birth. The day's work of the Blessed One is thus set forth in the Pāli books :

The Blessed One wakes up at two o'clock in the morning and sits in samādhi for His own happiness and in compassion for the world and seeks by His divine eye whether there is any one with the upanis-saya karma fit to receive the gift of Truth that day, and when he sees in any part of the world the person, whether he be god or man, He would go to the place in the natural way, if the place is within measurable distance of one or more yojana ; if the place is very far He would then use His iddhi power to transport Himself through space. The farthest world of many thousand million miles distance to Him was no distance. The time it takes for a strong man to stretch his arm is the time required for the Blessed One to visit the distant world of Brahmā. It is said that

28

from the sacred Body of the Biessed One there goes
out rays of glory always, and on certain occasions He
wills that they should emit several miles, and the
people accustomed to the process recognise them and
make preparations to receive the Blessed One. On
certain days He goes without the company of
Bhikkhus to receive alms from the people. The
wealthy Brahmans invite the Blessed One to their
homes together with the Bhikkhus in number about
twelve hundred. Before the sun passes the meridian
He finishes the day's meal, and for twenty four hours
there was only one meal which He partook, and He
strongly urged the Bhikkhus not to eat heavy food after
the sun passes the meridian. It was a help to keep
the body in good health as well as for psychical reasons
to develop the higher faculties. A little time after
the meal is over He would give individually to each
Bhikkhu instructions to develop the psychical insight
for the attainment of Nirvāna, according to the
upanissaya karma of each. The psychical temperament of each Bhikkhu He sees, and looks to the
Bhikkhu's past birth before instructions are given.
Some are inclined to lustful passion, some are muddle-
headed, some are hot headed, some have more of
faith, some have more reasoning power, some have
more virility, and by the variations of temperament

29

the individual Bhikkhu is judged, and the karmasthāna best suited to the development of the individual is given, and the Bhikkhu is intructed to go into a retreat far or near, or to the Himalayas.

In the afternoon laymen and laywomen visit the Buddha with sweet fragrance and flowers and offer them at His sacred feet. He instructs them in the duties of the householder about the consequences that follow the life of sense enjoyment, about renunciation and purification. If the Blessed One sees the receptive heart in the listener He would then preach the "sāmukkansika dhamma". viz., the Four Noble Truths. In the afternoon the Blessed One bathes His body and engage in conversation with the incoming Bhikkhus from distant places and countries, and at ten o'clock the Bhikkhus all retire, when the Buddha sits alone till midnight to receive the visits from the heavenly beings. At midnight He retires to rest, and consciously repose on His right side to wake up again at two in the morning for the day's work.

Thus did the Blessed One spend the time for forty five years, counting it not by years and months but by hours. An hour is equal to one year according to the psychology of spiritual growth. The Blessed One reposed only two hours a day, and to His Bhikkhus

He gave four hours to sleep according to "Jāgariyānu-yoga". During the rainy season travelling is stopped, and the Bhikkhus were to remain in a place during the three months in one place. Where they stopped, especially in villages, they were fed by the village people. and the Bhikkhus preached daily to them. A programme for the whole year of activity was discussed at the pavārana ceremony which was in the month of Kartik (October). Some times the Blessed One during the rainy season retires into solitude with instructions given before hand that only one Bhikkhu who is to attend on Him, shall see Him.

In the first assembly of Bhikkhus held at Rājagriha under the Blessed One in the seventh month after His Enlightenment there were 1250 Arhats.

In the tenth month after the Enlightenment the Blessed One left Rajagriha with a retinue of about 20,000 to His father's kingdom, and at Kapilavastu the elderly Sakyan princes were reluctant to pay homage to Him, and the Blessed One to break down their "Sakyan" pride showed the "Double Miracle" (yamaka pātihariya) and received their homage led by the aged Rājā Suddhodana. He is no prophet who does not receive the homage of his own people.

No man, god, angel or demon can kill a Buddha. This is a law. The best of the Brahman thinkers joined

31

the yellow robe and became Arhats. The two chief
disciples of the Buddha were of the Brahman clan,
Sāriputra and Moggallāna. Within the Holy Order
of the Yellow Robe there was no distinction of caste.
All were admitted and they were known as the
"Sakyaputra Sramanas". The Buddha addressed the
people in the purified Māgadhi language.

To the householders the Blessed One taught the
four principles of Service, viz :, Dāna, priyavacana,
samānātmatā and artha chariya. Dāna is universal all
comprehensive charity ; priyavacana is sweet speech ;
samānātmatā is equality in treatment ; arthachariya is
a life usefulness for the good of others. The ethical
principle of Universal brotherhood was thus spiritually
established.

The Blessed One taught history, social ethics, old
world stories, kindness to animals, communal service,
the duties of the king to his people, the duties of the
Brahmans, about the duties of the wife to the husband,
about the law of cause and effect, about rebirth in
heavens, in the animal womb, in the different hells for
the sins committed, about giving release to the
departed who are born in the preta loka, about the
evolution of the embryo, about observing caste rules
to keep the kulavanse (social rank) and not depart from
the laws laid down by ancestors.

The life of holiness was enunciated according to grades viz., the sotāpatti, the sakadāgāmi, anāgāmi and the highest, arhat.

Hells, pretalokas, animal kingdom, human kingdom, celestial regions, the heavens of the purified gods, the heavens of no perception, the heaven of pure consciousness, the formation of the solar systems, their number going up to billions, the formation of the earth from the nebular state, the growth of primeval life, the origin of the first life wave, the origin of the myth of the creator, the forty different methods to obtain happiness by means of purification of the mind, the superiority of mind and its growth when associated with the law of meritorious activity, the retardation of its growth when led by ignoble desires, the development of ideal desires, about the despicable ways of the householder, and the way that he should live to enjoy happiness, the methods to be employed to develop arts, industries, agriculture, cattle keeping, dairying and trade—all these and a hundred other subjects He taught to the people of India.

The Buddha proclaimed a complete doctrine of the past present and future. There is no known beginning, and no end. Nothing is created, and, nothing can be annihilated, and there is no permanent thing in the universe. Everything is subject to

C

change. Those questions that are set aside are called thapaniya, and those questions that can't be answered are called Abyākatā. The condition of Nirvāna is abyākatā, beyond speech. Nirvāna is a condition to be realized, and words and verbal explanations can never describe the state of Nirvāna. Questions that are outside the pale of the Nirvāna doctrine are the following :—

Is the world eternal ? Is the world not eternal ? Is the world finite ? Is the world not finite ? Is the Jiva the same as the body ? Is the Jiva another and the body another ? Does the being exist after death ? Does the being not exist after death ? Does the being exist and cease to exist after death ? The being does not exist and will not exist after death ? Are the world and the atman eternal ? the world and the atman not eternal ? Are the world and the atman eternal and also not eternal ? Was the soul as well as the world self made ? Was the soul made by another as well as the world ? Were they both self made and also made by another ? Were they not self made ; and made not by another and yet began at a certain time without a cause ?

According to the Blessed One these are theories, and the Blessed One is free from dogmatic expressions. He is a vibhajjavādi an Analyst, not a dogmatist (ekamsavādi). The theory in connection with these dogmas is a jungle, a wilderness, a puppet show, a writhing, and a fetter and is coupled with misery, ruin despair, and agony, and does not tend to aversion, absence of passion, cessation, quiescence, knowledge, supreme wisdom and Nirvāna. There is no place in the practical doctrine of the Buddha for speculative theories. He is the physician and the surgeon, and He found that man suffers from Ignorance and Covetousness, and that he is vacillating between fear and scepticism. When Naciketa asked Yama the question does the soul of man exist after death, or does not exist after death, the answer that Yama gave was : Naciketa do not put such a question for it is not decided by the gods. The Blessed One after having gained Omniscience found that there is neither a permanency nor an annihilation of existence ; but a continuous change depending on the law of cause and effect according to the good or evil karma.

In enunciating the doctrine of karma the Blessed One gave the immortal doctrine of ceaseless activity for mortals to live up to. Aim high and exert strenuously to reach the goal of non-anger, non lust and enlightenment. Appamāda and Virya were the two great principles that the Blessed One ceaselessly proclaimed. For fortyfive years, from the 35th year to the 80th year the Blessed One worked for the happiness of the world of gods and men. In the 80th year The Blessed One finished His work and on the full moon day of Baisakh, He entered into the anupādhi sesa nibbāna dhātu at Kusinārā in the Sāla Grove of the Mallyan princes.

THE DHARMAKAYA OF THE BLESSED ONE, THE BUDDHA.

At one time The Blessed One, the Buddha, was staying at Sāvatthi in the Eastern Vihāra, called the Palace of Migāra's mother.

The two young Brahman Sāmaneras, Vāsettha and Bhāradvāja, expecting full ordination into the Holy Order of Bhikkhus were staying in the Vihāra with the company of Bhikkhus.

The young Brahmans were accomplished in the three Vedas, and of noble birth, inheritors of great wealth.

And the Blessed One having arisen from the meditation called phala samāpatti, in which state He realizes the bliss of solitude, and leaving the Vihāra, went to the place where the Cloister was, which stood under the shade of the shadow of the Vihāra.

And the Blessed One was walking up and down, and from His golden complexioned body there went forth the six-coloured rays.

At this time the Brahman youths saw at a distance the Blessed One walking to and fro the shaded Cloister, and the Brahman Vesattha said to the young Brahman Bhāradvāja.

Look, there is the Blessed One the Buddha, walking to and fro the cloister. Let us go down and meet the Holy One.

Peradventure the Holy One will be graciously pleased to deliver a discourse, which will be to our advantage.

And the young Brahman Bharadvāja assented, and they came to where the Blessed One was walking, and—

They approached the Blessed One and made Him obeisance, and followed the footsteps of the Blessed One, to and fro the cloister.

Thereupon the Blessed One addressing them by name said well, Vāsettha, Brahmans by birth ye are, thou and Bhāradvāja, belonging to families of high birth, and now ye have forsaken the wealth that is thine, and entered the Religion of Noble Discipline.

What do the Brahmans say ? Do they use harsh words to show thee their displeasure, and do they blame thee ?

Lord, they do blame and use harsh words and abuse us and despise us most vehemently.

And the Blessed One inquired and said, in what way do the Brahmans speak ill of thee, and blame thee Vāsettha ?

Lord, Holy One, vouchsafe to hear what the Brahmans say, and Vaseṭṭha began :

The Brahmans alone belong to the high caste, the other castes are low ; only the Brahmans are pure ; other castes are impure, the Brahmans are by birth sons of Brahmā, the Brahmans repose in the bosom of Brahmā, from the mouth of Brahmā came forth the Brahmans, and Brahmā created them, and the Brahmans are the inheritors of Brahmā, they are born of Brahmā.

And this high inheritance ye hath renounced and have accepted the low born position of the blacks, off scourings of the feet of Brahmā, despised are the low-born, and ye have gone forth and joined the despised shavelings. Great indeed is the wrong ye hath done.

Holy One the Brahmans in this wise do blame us and slander the holy Bhikkhus.

And the Blessed One thereupon said, Vāseṭṭha, it seemeth the Brahmans have forgotten the ancient story of the birth of the world, which was known to the Ancients, and therefore do they blame thee and the non Brahmans, and use slanderous language and condemn them that do not belong to their caste.

Now Vāseṭṭha, give ear and listen, and the Blessed One, said

The Brahmans for the sake of getting issue, bring

39

women of marriageable age, of the Brahman caste, and also do give their daughters to Brahmans, and their women are seen during the period of menstruation, and in the period of pregnancy, and the time when they are going to give birth, and their women are seen when giving their breasts to suck the babes. All this is seen.

And the Brahmans nevertheless declare, although born of women that the Brahmans are superior in caste, and the non-Brahmans are low, the Brahmans are white and the non-Brahmans are black, that Brahmans are holy and others are impure, the Brahmans are sons of Brahmā produced from the bosom of Brahmā, born out of the mouth of Brahmā, created by Brahmā, and are inheritors of Brahmā. All this is seen.

And yet the Brahmans born of women in declaring themselves sons of Brahmā say things which are utterly false. In saying that the Brahmans came out of the mouth of Brahmā they defame Brahmā, and in slandering Brahmā and speaking falsely they create and accumulate sin.

And the Blessed One continued and said, Vāsettha, there are four categories of human beings, those of the landholder caste, of the Brahman caste, of the trading class, and those of the serving caste.

And among the landholder caste there are some
who commit sin by the destruction of life, by illicit
gain, by unlawful sexual intercourse, by uttering falsehood, by slandering others, by using harsh words by
unprofitable conversation, by covetous desires, by
showing hatred to others by harbouring erroneous
views contrary to truth ;

And these things which are considered sinful,
which belong to the category of evil, which should be
avoided, declared as evil, unfit to be practised by the
noble disciple, which have been condemned as sinful
and producing sorrow, and despised by the wise,

And these sins are seen as being committed by
some of the landholder caste, and by some of the
Brahman caste, and by some of the Vaishya caste, and
by some in the serving class ;

And Vāsettha, in this world, are found some
among the landholder caste who abstain from the
destruction of life, and other aforesaid evils, and live
the righteous life ; and also among the Brahman class
some are found following the path of righteousness,
and also among the Vaishya and the Sudra some are
found who walk in the path of righteousness, praised
by the wise.

And Vāsettha, the saying of the Brahmans that
only among the Brahmans are found the high,, and the

41

rest are low, and that the Brahmans alone came out of the mouth of Brahmā, and that they are inheritors ef Brahmā ;

Such a saying, Vāsettha, is not approved of by the wise and among the four categories of human beings, whomsoever hath attained the path of the highest holiness of Arhatship, hath destroyed all evil desires, hath lead the godly life, hath walked in the four paths, hath done all things which hath to be done, hath laid aside the burden of contaminating evils, hath realized the consummation of Self, hath destroyed the burden of Existence.

Such a one Vāsettha may be called the Superman, by righteousness not by unrighteousness.

Vāsettha, in this world and in the next, Truth (Dhamma) alone is supreme.

It hath been said that Pasenadi, king of Kosala, knows that the Sramana Gautama of the Sākya clan hath gone forth leaving home to become an ascetic.

It hath been declared that the Sakyans pay tribute to the King of Kosala, and that they obey his laws.

And the elderly Sakyans show their respect to the king, and the younger Sakyans pay homage to the King by bringing the two palms together.

And the King doth receive the respect of the eleder

Sakyans, and the homage of the younger Sakyans, and

This King when he sees the Tathāgata, the Buddha, pays obeisance, homage and worship to the Blessed One, saying

The Buddha is well born, I the king am not ; the Blessed One is full of strength, I the king am not ; the sight of the Blessed One pleaseth the heart, my complexion is not pleasing ; the Sramana Gautama is full of power, I the king am not.

In this wise doth the King sing the praise of the Blessed One.

The King in paying honour to Truth doth honour the Tathgāata.

Vāsettha ¡ Truth alone is supreme, both here and in the world to come.

Vāsettha, all ye that hath entered the Noble Order of Discipline, ye are of different castes and belong to different castes, and hath left home and joined the Holy Order of the Homeless.

And whensoever any one asketh what are ye, whose following are ye, Do ye say, We are the disciples of the Sramana Sākyaputra.

Vāsettha, Know ye that he who hath unshakable faith in the Tathāgata, deeply rooted, not be disturbed

by a Brahman, god, Māra, or Brahmā or by any person
in the world ;

He may be called as one born in the Aryabhumi.
and as living in association with the Tathāgata, and he
is called Son of the Blessed One, born of His Word,
and the well beloved son, born of Truth, created by
Truth, inheritor of Truth.

The Tathāgata out of His own mind created the
Dhamma. The Body of the Tathāgata is created by
Truth, and it is called the Body of Truth and is the
Supreme Body.

44

EXHORTATIONS OF THE BLESSED ONE TO KINGS.

India had always her own kings before the Moslem invasion, which took place in the last decade of the 10th century of the Christian Era. Previous to the Moslem invasion no foreign foe desecrated the hallowed soil of India.

About 2220 years ago Alexader invaded the country now known as Candahar. But he did not come over to India proper. For nearly a thousand years India has remained dependent on the foreign conquerors. The first great name that occurs in Indian Puranic history is Ikhsvaku of the solar dynasty. From the line of Ikhsvaku the descent of the Buddha is traced. The Vishnu Purāna gives the name of the Suryavansa kings beginning from Iksvaku, and in the list is mentioned the name of King Suddhodana. The Sakya clan occupied the territory north of Kosala. The Buddha was the teacher of King Bimbisāra of Magadha and of Pasenadi King of Kosala. King Bimbisāra's son, Ajātasatru at first was against the Blessed One, but later on became a faithful disciple, and helped the early Apostles of the Buddhist Church and became the patron of the first convocation held at Saptaparni Cave at the Vebhāra Rock at Rajagriha. The King of Kosala till death remained a fervant disciple of the Blessed One, but his successor the Prince Vidudabha massacred the Sakyans of Kapilavastu.

The Blessed One in the Cakkavatti Sutta of the Digha Nikāya enunciated the political principles of good government which formed the bases of the primitive Aryan administration. The king was known as Dhammaraja ruling according to the ethics of righteous government. The symbol of the ever revolving wheel was the symbol of Aryan government. Ariya Cakkaratana had power to promulgate the laws of righteous government. What did the Ariya Chakkavatti proclaim ?

Do not destroy life.

Do not steal.

Do not commit adultery.

Do not tell lies.

Do not drink intoxicating liquor.

Protect and nurse Mother and Father and the Elders of the Family

The King was taught to follow the principles of Dhamma, and to make righteousness the basis of good government. The King has to see that his subjects are not reduced to poverty. He must rule the people of his kingdom in righteousness, and look to the welfare of his army, of the Khattiyas, Brahmans and householders of the towns and villages and provinces, of the holy sramanas and holy Brahmans and of the fourfooted beasts and birds, and let no unrighteousness prevail in his kingdom If there are in the kingdom people who are poor, let them be given the means to obtain wealth, and by exertion when wealth is obtained let the people be exhorted to take care of their parents. sons and wives, to engage in some kind of art or craft, give charity to the yellow robed Sramanas and the holy Brahmans, things necessary for their welfare, so that heaven may be obtained in reward whereof. In the Sāmaññaphala sutta, Dighanikaya, the Blessed One enunciated the principle of democrate spirituality which is higher than the ethics of royal service. In the Aggañña sutta, the Blessed One showed that in Aryan society the king was elected by the people, and that the king is called Rājā because he has to delight the hearts of the people. In the Mahāparinibāna sutta, Dighanikāya, the Blessed One enunciated the seven principles of political unity, which should be followed by smaller states if they wish to keep their independence. The king is responsible for the prevalence of crime in his kingdom. When the king

47

falls from the exalted state of righteousness, his ministers become corrupt, and Brahmans become unrighteous, and crime prevails.

The king should fulfil the laws of righteousness so that the people will follow him in the path of virtue. He must practice, charity, open alms houses, and take care of the holy men in his kingdom be, kind in his speech, treat every one with equal tenderness and make his reign a righteous one.

The best example of a Buddhist king is the great Emperor Asoka, and after two thousand years the world has come to realize the wonderful deeds he had done for the prosperity of the people over whom he ruled. The rock cut edicts of the King "Beloved of the gods" speak to-day to the whole world what a king's duties are.

With the extinction of the Kshattriya kings in India, state support was withdrawn which was given to the maintenance of scholarly Bhikkhus and their pupils. Aliens and low caste kings showed no sympathy with the yellow robed Bhikkhus, and when they found no support they had to leave the country. Buddhism is like a tender plant that requires nursing. When the ruling king turns bad the Bhikkhus follow the exhortation of the Blessed One ; they leave his kingdom. For a thousand years the law of righteousness has remained dormant. May the time soon come when the Law of Piety will reign in the heart of the people and the princes of India.

THE ETHICS OF THE HAPPY HOME

The Blessed One began His mission of Love and
Wisdom with the announcement of the gift of
Immortality to those who were willing to listen to the
Noble Doctrine of Eternal Freedom from Sin and
Sorrow ; from Hatred and Lust and from Ignorance.

The Blessed One wished that all living beings
should enjoy the bliss of peace, and happiness.

For seven weeks after the realization of the
Wisdom under the Bodhi Tree at Uruvela near the
river Neranjarā, the Blessed One sat at seven places
in the enjoyment of (vimutti sukha) the happiness of
emancipation. He psychologically thought out the
complex ramifications of the twenty four laws based
on 24 Causes. The whole universe was brought
under one great Law. Every phenomenon has a
Cause (ye dhammā hetu pabhavā) and this Cause the.
Tathāgato has explained. The kaleidoscopic operations of the 24 laws the Tathāgata witnessed, and it is
said that when the whole scene became manifest to
the mind's eye of the Blessed One, that there went
forth from His glorified body the six coloured rays of
blue, yellow, red, white, crimson and a blending of

THE ETHICS OF THE HAPPY HOME.

the five in one ray which coalesced with the other waves travelling to the remotest limits of the universe.

The consummation of His desires, the peace of absolute Nirvana He realized, and now comes the Tempter, Māra, the chief God of the pleasurable heavens, and solicits the Blessed One to enjoy the bliss of Peace in solitude, alone, without any kind of active display. Live in Peace, why make the effort, said Māra. The Blessed One answered "Evil One, Friend of Death, thy prayer shall not be answered. The rest and the peace which thou want that I should enjoy alone shall not be mine till I see the whole world become partakers thereof. Not until the company of Bhikkhus, Bhikkhunis, Upāsakas and Upāsikās (monks, nuns, laymen and laywomen) is formed, and properly equipped in my Doctrine, and able to subdue the heresies and able to proclaim the Noble Doctrine, shall the Tathāgata live in the enjoyment of Nirvanic repose. Away with thee Evil One."

The Doctrine is hard to understand thought the Blessed One. Men given to pleasurable enjoyments and living amidst luxury will they receive it ? Just then the cry was heard from the heavens "Lord the world is ready to receive the Doctrine, preach Lord and save the world." The God of Love, the Brahmā

51

Sahampati, the Lord of all gods, thus spake, and appeared before the Blessed One.

Buddhism does not believe in persecuting people for the sake of religion. The Buddha saw by His divine eye that there are three kinds of human beings, the fully blossomed, ready to bloom, and the buds that may bloom later. Men's minds are compared to the lotus flower in the three grades, *viz.*, the fully bloomed, the flower above water ready to blossom, snd the flower unopened yet under water. The boy in the lower class is not equal to the student in the middle form, and the senior student in the higher form is superior to both. It would be foolish to expect that the boy of the lower form could at once develop into the senior boy. Time is required to grow. This doctrine is emphasised in the Dharma of the Tathāgata. The human being was not created a clay idol and galvanised by the fiat of a bloodthirsty demon-god. He is the product of his own karma. Man and animal, have no known beginning. There is no beginning in the cosmology of Buddhism. The beginning can't be found, because there is no known beginning. It is eternity behind, and eternity. beyond. There is nothing permanent and nothing can be annihilated. Only the law of change endures. Countless billions of solar systems exist, the whole universe is spiritually bound by the law of cause and effect.

Until the last dying moment there is hope for the better in the case of man. There must not be any show of impatience to compel him to do anything against his will. Kindly, lovingly, persuade him to be good, if he is going in the path of self-destruction, which also means that he is bringing unhappiness on others. No man can do evil for himself alone. He who does good to himself helps others. Besides the Blessed One saw that each individual has his own upanissaya karma, and to force him to do a thing when he has not the potentiality to grasp it, would be going against the law of karma. You can't make the thistle to produce figs. The mango tree will only produce mango, not coconuts.

The Blessed One enunciated the laws of Heredity, the germinating power of the Seed, the operating cause, and the Law of Nature. (kamma, bija, utu, dhamma). Buddhism knows no persecution, or oppression on religious or psychological grounds. There is all eternity before you, therefore why fear of annihilation ? The compassion of the Buddhas is due to their Wisdom, and they wish to save those who are ready to hear the good. So long as there is eternity before there will be a line of

Buddhas in continuity preparing Humanity for the acceptance of the Dhamma of the future Buddhas. The world will never be devoid of Holy Men.

The Blessed One wished to make the Aryan home happy. He wished to make the wife a goddess and the husband a god.

The Blessed One wished to make the city beautiful, with its gardens, parks, tanks, forests, the alms hall, the public bath, the resting hall, the hospital, the townhall, the retreat for the religious, the lying in home, the beautiful ārāma with its park, pavilion, tank, night station, day station, cloister, hot bath, dining hall, service hall, garden of flowers, garden of fruits, and with this end in view He trained the Bhikkhus to become the teachers of the old and the young.

The perfections of virtue He taught to the householder. He must learn to give charity, however little, daily. He should train himself in the science of giving. Even a grain of rice the householder must learn to give. Morality is a necessity, it is the foundation of domestic happiness. No man who is a thief, will be admitted into respectable society. Man is a social, evolving, psychical being ; he can't live without company. He must have his relations to make him happy. The man without friends, relations, wife and children would not be able to endure life. Gods do not come down daily to keep company with man, and must therefore learn to behave morally and socially for the happiness of others.

There are certain religions that teach the existence of only one god. That god must be very unhappy. A god without company is a prisoner. The prophet who presented that kind of god to the world did not consult the god's happiness, except his own. He perhaps wished to be the despot and he duped the people to believe in one god. The poor god must be pitied. He has only to be satisfied with the little blood that is given to him, and to see that the prophet gets all that he requires in the shape of more women, more liquor, more meat. An all powerful God is a psychological monstrosity. Progressive Evolution repudiates it. Barbaric paganism accepts it.

The people of ancient India did not fear the gods. Gods and men were not inimical to each other. They were interdependent. A blood-thirsty fiend in the form of a jealous god had no existence in the Aryan pantheon. The Supreme Law of Truth and Righteousness was above the gods ; and no one dared to disobey the Great Law. The prophets who proclaimed the doctrine of a despotic god had no idea of the great Eternal Law of Cause and Effect,

In the Ethics of the Happy Home which the Blessed One enunciated there was no place for a despotic god who goeth against immutable laws. The gospel of self help is the profound doctrine which the Buddha proclaimed. To do the will of a Creator means to conform to the foolishness of a pagan prophet who proclaimed the idea. There is no place in the Law of Righteousness for the equally despicable dogma of Fatalism. The foolish idea that man has been preordained to go through suffering, destroys the power of rational activity which is the birth right of the individual with a consciousness. The mind has no other work to do, but to generate Sankhāras, and when it is associated with wisdom begotten of science, there is no place for the fatalistic idea of predestination. A despotic creator and a dogma asserting that man is fated to go through a predestinated course rob man of his power to individualised activity in harmony with the law of Cause and Effect. Equally despicable is the dogma that man had no past and has no future, and that at death of the physical body, existence ceases. These were the beliefs of the Animists of ancient India.

To believe in the semitic dogma that man was

made out of the dust of the ground connotes that he had no past, and that life began at a certain period, and that there is no more life after the death of the physical body. Such a doctrine is only fit for the Bedouin of the waterless desert.

Dr. Flinders Petrie in his most interesting work called the *Dawn of Civilization*, gives a picture of an ancient Egyptian piece of sculpture, where the god *Khnumu* is shown modelling man upon a potter's table. The ancient Egyptian idea of God making man from clay was incorporated in the later Semitic religions which had their foundation in the extreme west coast of Asia.

The greatness of man consists in his indomitable will to do good, and the power to realize Truth by his own self-sacrificing efforts. Rob man of this great virtue and he degenerates into a savage with the instincts of the tiger and the hyena.

Certain countries are by nature unsuited for agriculture, and in countries where people are engaged in rice cultivation, nature helps them to acquire wisdom by the experience of the daily efforts they are making to prepare the soil to sow the seed. The agriculturist has to observe, when the season arrives for sowing, meteorological changes in the atmosphere. He observes the gradual changes that

57

are taking place when the seed of the rice begins to germinate. He values the efforts he makes to get a good harvest ; he values the labour of the oxen without whose help he could not plough the field. In agricultural countries where rice is the staple food of man, it is remarkable that the idea of a Creator never found acceptance. It is the Bedouin and the wandering savage and the pirate who prays to a deity to protect him from danger while he is plundering and murdering others.

The Happy Home of the Aryan was not converted into a butcher's slaughter house. He did not contaminate the life giving earth with the blood of innocent and helpless victims whom he ruthlessly slaughtered to satisfy his lust. And he did not invoke an infuriated god as his authority to spill innocent blood. The Aryan began with the slogan his day's work "ahimsāparamodharmah". Mercy is the supreme law. And the God that the Aryan worshipped had the four attributes of Love. Compassion, Delight and Equal mindedness. And the God was called Brahmā. The Earth was not cursed by the Aryan gods. They blessed it, The idea of a god cursing the earth is too revolting to contemplate. It is the consummation of the Gospel of Curse.

The Ethics of the Happy Home inculcated certain duties on the family. The chief of the family was called the Ariya sāvaka and he was honoured with the appellation of deva, and the obedient wife was called devi. The Aryan householder had to listen to the Good Law, and he had to also to think rationally from cause to effect. There were certain things which he had to abandon as they were contaminations (kamma kilesā) ; certain things he had to abstain from doing (pāpa kamman nakaroti) ; certain things that led him towards hell he had to dissociate with (apāya mukhāni nasevati).

The contaminating acts are killing, stealing, committing adultery, enjoying sense pleasures ignobly, and lying speech.

The good Aryan must not be guided by his prejudices ; anger, fear and ignorance he must avoid.

The immoralities that lead a man to hell are Intoxication, wandering from place to place at unusual hours ; attending bacchanalian orgies ; association with evil companions and addicted to indolent habits.

The happiness of the householder is lost if he is given to drinking intoxicating liquor. The Blessed One enumerated the following evils resulting from drunkennes :

Immediate loss of wealth ; getting entangled in quarrels, and provoking them ; prepares the body for new diseases ; loss of reputation ; looses the sense of shame ; deteriorates the thinking faculty and helps to arrest the mental growth. In the next life he suffers from insanity.

The ethic of the Happy Home enjoins on the householder certain duties which are compulsory. He has to take care of his parents ; his sons and wife ; he has to attend to his friends and ministers, and to his servants and craftsmen, and to the holy ascetics (samanas and holy Brahmanās. He has to give his sons education in arts, sciences (silpa, karmānta, vidyā and karma), and he has to look after the wants of the teacher who teaches his sons. He must be true to his friend, and take care of him when he is in danger, must not abandon him when he is in want, and even he should be prepared to sacrifice his own life for the true friend. He has to divide his income into four parts, and spend one portion for his own comforts, two portion he has to set apart for his livelihood, and one portion he must lay aside as a provident fund. From the portion that he spends for his own use he should daily give a tenth portion for charity.

The Aryan householder if he is to live happily

never should show slothfulness at any time. The indolent man loses what he has in his possession, and is
never able to gain new wealth.

Indolence is the path to hell, and the wise man
should think that activity is immortality (appamādo
amatapadam).

Four things the Aryan householder should cultivate viz., charity, (dāna) ; sweet speech (priya vacana)
equal treatment to all (samāna ātmatā); and social
service (arthachariyā).

For forty five years the Blessed One exhorted
daily the Upāsakas and the Upasikās of Aryavarta.
The representative Husband and Wife of the Aryan
Home are like the two Wheels of the Chariot. They
must be alike in the nobility of their conduct, in their
Wisdom and in their attachment to each other.
Nakulapitā and Nakulamātā are the best examples of
the Aryan husband and Aryan wife.

———

THE PATH OF PSYCHOLOGY.

The Buddha preached the Dhamma as well as a higher Dhamma. The latter is called the Abhidhamma. The Dhamma contains the popular Doctrine explained in a popular way the path to heaven, to the Brahmā lokas and also to Nirvāna.

The pure Brahman philosophy untainted by the doctrine of egohood is in no way antagonistic to the Dhamma of the Tathāgata. Pure Brahmanism became contaminated after the religion of the Buddha Kasyapa had disappeared. The purifying doctrine was again preached by the Buddha Gotama.

The essence of the Religion of the Buddhas is "Avoid all evil ; increase the sum totality of good deeds ; unceasingly cleanse the heart : this is the religion of the Buddhas,"

The Tathāgatas are the preachers of the supreme doctrine of *anātma*, which is synonymous with the word Nirvāna. Nirvāna is a condition to be created by self control, wisdom and love. Anger, illwill, hatred, pride, conceit, indolence, delay in doing the right thing, slothfulness, desire to do evil, exhibiting the spirit of revenge, desire to enjoy unhealthy lustful pleasure, harbouring anger, scepticism, self esteem, hypocrisy, running down others, covetousness, arrogance, stubborness, unyielding to truth, showing partiality, fear, muddleheadness etc., are obstacles to the realization of Nirvanic happiness.

There is a path to realize the supreme condition of Nirvāna, and that path is reached by the fulfilment of the ten pāramitas, viz., unbounded charity ; purity in body by avoiding killing, stealing, committing adultery, speaking falsehood, drinking intoxicating liquor, smoking or eating stupefying drugs ; desire to practise the higher life of sexual purity, avoiding sensuality ; making efforts to acquire the higher wisdom ; ever exerting in the performance of righteous duty ; never deviating from the path of truthfulness ; always willing to forgive even when persecuted and tortured ; strengthening the will power by making good resolutions and keeping them even at the risk of life ; showing love to all living beings, visible and invisible ; and always contented and cheerful whatever happens. These ten pāramitas have to be practised by those who wish to reach the haven of Nirvāna. The Haven of Nirvāna may be reached in three ways, viz., by the abhisambodhi method, by the pratyeka bodhi method, and by the srāvaka bodhi method. The pāramitas must be practised by the first method for four, eight or sixteen asankhya kalpas ; the second method requires two asankheyya kalpas, and the last, one asankheyya. The name given to those who practise the parami path is Bodhisatva and the candidate to Buddhahood is called Mahasatva.

The Buddha after His enlightment enunciated the Middle Path for laymen and Bhikkhus to enter Nirvāna within the period that His Dhamma lasts viz., five thousand years. There are four paths under His Dispensation to reach the Nirvāna goal. The sotā-patti, sakadāgāmi, anāgāmi, and arahatta, The laymen may follow the sotāpatti, sakadāgāmi and anāgāmi paths. The arahat path is for the Bhikkhus not for householders. In the dispensation of the Gautama Buddha the path was made so easy that if one most strenuously exerts he can reach Nirvāna here on this earth, in this life within a limited period, ranging from one day to seven years, but the most strenuous will, unceasing effort day and night, night and day is needed.

The goal when once reached, experiencing the bliss of Nirvāna is the same with the Buddha and the Arhats. The Buddha is the first Discoverer of the path long hidden, and He then tells the world of the existence of the great palace which is the end, and all must make the effort. The inventor of the motor car had to go through all the painful work before he obtained the results, but once he arrived at the goal of success, the path is easy, and the manufacturing of the motor car becomes easy.

Every individual living being is eternal, without a beginning and without end. There are two ways of existence the going round and round the circle like the bullock yoked to the mill with its eyes bandaged, now enjoying, now under going misery, now in hell now in heaven, now being born in the Brahmaloka, now an animal ; and the eternal round of weary sansāra continues to be the easy way to the ignorant, muddle headed being. Like the sorrow stricken man who takes to drinking intoxicating liquor to forget his misery, the ignorant man goes round and round the weary circle under the opiate of sense pleasures, false beliefs, and scepticisms. The savage never thinks of the future, he is satisfied if he gets some thing to eat and drink, and a place to lie down.

The Aryan people of India had a most spiritualizing code of ethics for several thousands of years. The Brahman, Kshatriya, and Vaishya philosophers of ancient India had penetrated into the heights of the Brahmalokas, and there found that the gods were most kind, compassionate, loving, and contented and living in joyousness. The calm atmosphere of the Himalaya mountains gave the philosophers an impetus for higher thought. They soared and found that the highest happiness can be secured only by practising the divine qualities of *mettā*, *karunā*, *muditā* and *upekkhā*. Love to all living beings, visible and invisible, far and near, high and low, devil and god, animal and man, all must be loved. Here the Aryan transcends all other nations. This is why India never is entirely destroyed.

The Buddha, 2500 years ago, came to show the Aryan to transcend to greater heights of altruistic freedom, and the teaching did elevate them, and the cultured Aryans left the shores of India for the distant countries to civilize and humanize the less civilized races. They carried the teachings of love, compassion, mercy, contentment, right thinking, right livelihood, and taught the half civilized races to give up butchering animals and to cultivate love. Sensuality and morbid asceticism were condemned and spiritually modified to enjoy a clear consciousness. Sensualism, materialistic beliefs and wealth make man a brute. Pride, ambition to get more power, degenerates the individuals and the race, and woe be to the man or race that follows the diabolical path.

The science of psychology will open the eyes of

man to the power of his own potentialities, and he will try to work for the good of others, because it will bring his own development to quicker realization. The radiant mind is neglected and man leads a life of animal selfishness.

Man according to the Buddha is an everchanging being. For two consecutive moments he is not the same. With the knowledge of Abhidharma he may live in perfect safety enjoying the bliss of solitude and peace.

EVOLUTION AND CREATION.

In the Brahmajāla sutta of the Di'gha nikāya, the Blessed One classified the religious beliefs current in ancient India. All people did not follow the theory of a cosmic creation, with Brahmā as the chief. The fact that there were current in ancient India sixty-two different kinds of religious, beliefs, shows that ancient Indian people were remarkably tolerant of each other's religious views.

The Blessed One explained the variations of religious beliefs to His own disciples, and exhorted them to be neutral and to avoid religious disputations. He said that the Bhikkhus should not feel elated when the Tathāgata is praised : neither should they betray their angry feelings when they hear the Tathāgata blamed. They suffer if in either way they betray their feelings. They are in search of the great Gem, and petty tyrannies and worldly applause should not make them to deviate from the path for a second.

The Creator myth is condemned by the Buddha. Creation connotes a beginning. In the Buddha Dharma there is no known beginning, Before the beginning what was the Creator doing, and where did

he live ? A condition of things where there is no
water, earth, air, heat, light, and space is unthinkable.
If God rested on the waters who created the water,
and if God created the water, where did he live
before ?

Uncultured people are always very credulous.
Analysis of religious beliefs is only possible in a
country where there exist more than one religion. In
a country where the people hold to one view of
religion, there could not be any kind of conflict.
Confusion of tongues creates differentiation. In the
most primitive period there might have been one
language in a country. The Buddha is called
Tathāgata, which connotes a successor of a former
Buddha. Buddhas have in the past appeared, and
their number is innumerable. Instead of yugas and
years, the Buddhas calculated time by kalpas, and
the duration of a kalpa cannot be measured by
arithmetical calculation.

A mahākalpa has twenty minor kalpas, and a
mahākalpa goes through four periods decay, destruction, suspended animation, and re-formation. The
modern scientific view of a nebular hypothesis is in
conflict with the creation theory.

The Vedic Brahmans were not philosophers,
they were priests and sacrificers to gods, and they

were able to create gods whenever they were
required. Hence the avatar theory. The tribe of
Brahmans were exclusive, and they monopolised the
priestly profession to themselves. The scriptures
which they read were their own property, and they
interpreted them for their own advantage-

In course of time the Purānas were compiled,
suggesting thereby a historic foundation. The
compiler of the Purānas was Veda Vyāsa. He was a
great seer and compiled a work which may be called
the history of the ancients.

There are eighteen Purānas which are as follow :
—Brahmapurāna, padmapurāna, Vishnupurāna, Siva-
purāna, Bhāgavatapurāna, Nāradiyapurāna, Markan-
deyyapurāna, Agnipurāna, Bhavishyapurāna, Brahma-
vaivartapurāna, Lingapurāna, Varahāpurān, Skandha-
purāna, Vāmanapurāna, Kurmapurāna, Matsyapurāna,
Garudapurāna, Brahmāndapurāna.

The Purānas give descriptions of meetings held
by gods and to these meetings the rishis were
admitted. Each god had his say, and the others
listened attentively. There was no disputation and no
conflict, and each purāna gives the names of a number
of gods who took part in the symposium. In the
Brahmāndapurāna the following names appear as
having taken part in advancing their views :—

Saunaka, Suta Suka, Lomaharsha, Vāyu, Maher-
vara, Bhagavan, Brahmā, Dakshā, Umā, Virabhadra,
Mahadeva.

In the Vāyu purāna are found the following names
of inter-locutors :—
Suta, Suka, Lomaharsha, Vāyu, Bhagavan,
Brahmā, Vishnu, Daksha, Rudra, Umā, Mahesvara,
Sanatkumāra, Nārada, Brihaspati.

In the Brahmavaivarta Purāna the following
names appear :—Saunaka, Sautira, Nārāyana, Mahā-
deva, Brahmā, Sri Dharma, Mahalakshmi, Saraswati,
Sāvitri, Sankara, Bhagavan, Nārada, Siva, Daksha,
Gopikā, Surya, Brahman, Sri Krishna, Gangā, Rādhikā
Yama, Rati, Himālaya, &c.

In the Kurma purāna the following names appear :
—Romaharshana, Indradyumna, Bhagavan, Kurma,
Suta, Rishi, Muni, Vishnu, Brahmā, Menovā, Pulastya,
Himavā, Srideva, Dahksha, Kanyā, Visvamitra, Jama-
dagni, Vasu, Vasishta, Bhārajvāda, Kasyapa, Sri
Krishna, Brahmavishnu, Vyāsa, Markandeyya and
Isvara.

The Aryan consciousness was elevated by the
spirit of tolerance. Why shonld it not, when it had
all the advantages for progress The mighty Himalayas, and the majestic rivers, the great forests were

the associates of spiritual student. There was no
jealousy and hatred in the Aryan consciousness,

Dr. Lionel Barnett in his "Antiquities of India"
says in the preface, "the record of Indian history is
one of deepest fascination, and the utmost imagina-
tions of romance pale beside it. Indeed the civilization of India may be fitly compared to its marvellous
temples, in which every emotion of the soul is
expressed in plastic form with thrilling intensity."

The Puranas give variations of the genesis story
as understood by the compilers. The compilers
divided the periods into yugas to show that at least
they had some idea of the immensity of time, and how
small the Semitic gods appear to the Aryan mind in
as much as the very creators of the Semitic mythology
were creations of yesterday. The Puranic authors
computed time by yugas, and the four yugas made one
maha-yuga. The first of the four yugas was called the
satya yuge. To a maha-yuga period there were
4 320 000 solar years. Seventy one maha-yugas make
one manvantara, and a thousand maha-yugas make
one kalpa.

The Semitic gods were of small mind. They
had no idea of the existence of other countries and
other nations, and the rivers of Mesapotamia and
Mount Ararat and the few races that occupied the

72

Euphrates valley and the Sinai desert went to make up the world. The cross became the totem, and the flesh of certain animals were taboo. The blood was life and the soul to the nomadic gods. The most devout had to eat the flesh of the god and drink his blood. Cannibal psychology could not go beyond !

Folklore myths of animistic tribes weae accepted as religious truths, and the world has deteriorated for nearly two thousand years, so great had been the demoralizing influence of Semitic animism.

Before the birth of the Buddha Dharma, the ancient philosophers in India had speculated on every conceivable form of the divine. The rishis by their purity of life obtained knowledge to commune with the divine consciousness, and they formulated the belief in the arupa brahmaloka, where existence was prolonged to the extent of 84000 kalpas. The Prince Siddhartha realized this divine state by means of purified knowledge, but He found that 84000 kalpas was a drop in the ocean of Time. He wished for some thing to go beyond time and space, and the Doctrine of Nirvana was the result of His triumphant conquest over matter and mind.

The interpretation of myths and the making of hymns to anthropomorphic gods were being done by the priests and prophets. Something new, something greater, was wanted to enlighten the world and the Tathāgata enunciated the religion of Truths and the Wisdom of Nirvana. The birth and death of gods was a small matter. The world was created, and the world was resting on the back of the tortoise and the tortoise was resting on the elephant, and the elephant resting on nowhere : such were the kind of myths the people liked to hear. The spirit of God moved on the waters, and water was there before God.

The Tathagata said something new, and there was no mention of a creator and a beginning of the world in His Doctrine.

The usual way to light a dark place was by burning a lamp. The lamp required a wick and oil. Some one arrives and tells the people who were accustomed to burn the oil and the wick that a light can be obtained without the use of the oil and the wick. The light is shown, but the people refuse the radiant light because there is no oil and wick in the bulb. The Buddha similarly came to give the world a new light without the intermeddling of gods, priests and blood sacrifice. A clear consciousness is the one thing which must not be expected from animists. Blood, meat, intowicating drinks, sensual orgism go hand in hand with a creator.

The Creator myth is to be found in the Majjhima

Nikāya in the Brahmanimantaniya and Māratajjāniya suttas. The brief account as given in the Brahmajāla is given below :—

"Now there comes a time after a long period when the world goes into dissolution.

At the time when it is going through the process of destruction the life wave ceases, and living beings transmigrate and are born in the heaven of the radiant gods called Abhassara.

They are mind born eating the food of delight, with radiant bodies, travelling through space, and in this happy condition they exist for ages.

And after a long period this world again begins to reintegrate, and in the re-evolution of the world the beings that were living in the Abhassara world cease to exist there and are reborn here. The first to be reborn here from the Radiant world is alone and he thinks "would that other beings might come to join me in this place, and with the thought instantaneously other beings from the radiant world are reborn here. The first born then thinks to himself" I am Brahmā, supreme, the mighty, the all seeing, the ruler, the Lord of all, the maker, the Creator &c. These that are here are born from me, and I created them.

In the Kevadda sutta Dighanikāya appear another version of the creator story, but with a sweet humour that makes every one smile. The Creator is to put to the test by a Bhikkhu, and Brahmā acknowledges his ignorance that he is not able to say when the creation will cease. The creator is unable to tell the end of his own creation !

In the Brahmanimantaniya sutta, the Buddha himself goes to the seat of Brahmā, and says : "Brahma, in saying that all things are permanent thou dost only declare thine own ignorance".

In that story Mãra stands near Brahmā and pleads on the latter's behalf, and the Buddha asked Brahmā to look back to some untold ages in the past and Brahmā confess his inability to look back so far !

Neither the authors of the creator myths nor the people to whom these myths were proclaimed knew anything of the formation of earth by slow degrees. Geology and astronomy they knew not. Muddle-headed they were ; and ignorant people were made victims of priestly selfishness.

In the Maha bodhi Jātaka, No 528, is also a refutation of the creator theory-

In the Dhammadhaja, Jātaka, No. 220, the Brahman is made to do the impossible. The Bodhisatta was in that life born in a Brahman family, and the King's captain is angry with him, and he makes the king to kill the Brahman by asking the Brahman

76

EVOLUTION AND CREATION.

to do what the captain himself thought was beyond
the power of gods. The ancient Indian people
believed that gods had power to create inorganic
things, "not even a deity can make a man with all
four virtues, and the four virtues are, not to envy, not
to drink wine, to have no low desire, and no wrath."

THE PSYCHOLOGY OF HEARING.

Man first hears and then he begins to think, and he thinks either in a way which may be called the right way or the wrong way. The Blessed One said "Bhikkhus, the sound and words that comes from outside, which he hears makes man to think, and he thinks either rationally or irrationally ' Para toca ghoso ayonisoca manasikāro, micchādi*tt*hi, para toca ghosoyonisoca manasikāro, sammādi*tt*hi''. Anguttara Nikāya.

All are born in the same way. The pain of travail makes no distinction between the woman of high caste and low caste ; the high and the low has to go through the same pain. The baby born whether of the high caste or low caste has to go through the same experience. Both are helpless, lying on its back it has to be fed by the mother, and for several months it can only croak, and the time comes when it begins to crawl, and until it is able to articulate, it is more like a baby animal utterly helpless. The baby left to itself when able to crawl, the first it does is to scratch the earth and eat it. It has no idea of taste except that of the taste of milk. In

the child state there is no differentiation of birth and
caste. Children in the infant state do not show the
spirit of ahamhāra, and are unable to assert their
individuality. When they begin to hear words, and
able to understand their meaning, and know that the
words come from their parents, and have to be
listened to, the sense of fear of punisshment begins.
When the sense of perception is developed, they
begin to distinguish colours. The sense of viññāna
begins when the child is able to drive away crows. At
this stage the age of discipline begins. Children of
tender age like to taste whatever is eatable, and they
like to hide the things they like for future use. Children
begin stealing at an early age. They receiving a
warning first, and then punishment.

Tec Aggañña sutta tells us that at the first dawn of
the world man was a spiritual being, eating no solid
food, satisfied with the light of his own effulgence,
and feeling no want of the light of the sun. The
future human being does he not go through this
experience for nearly ten months in the womb of the
mother ? The story as related in the Aggañña sutta
is more like an allegory of the birth of the embryo, its
development in the womb, the coming out of the
womb fully grown, its first feeling of darkness, its first
cry, and then its first experience of seeing the sun

light, the first tasting of milk, and later on when it begins to crawl, milk is substituted for some kind of soft food. At this stage it begins to eat earth and dirt etc. If the story is carefully read in the light of an allegory it will be found that the Buddha wished to provoke the intelligent mind to think how foolish and sinful it is to think that man was created, and that he is superior to another by reason of mere birth. The story is an allegory of the evolution of the embryo and the rebirth of consciousness.

The caste feeling is artificial. The theory of caste is taught to the Brahman boy in his twelfth year. The colour feeling is also transmitted in European countries from the parent to the child. The child first hears and he is taught to carry out the order of his parents or teacher or priest. According to the Brahmanical Puranas the theory of caste was enunciated in the Dvāparayuga ; in the Satya and Treta age there was no caste.

Why do grown up men do evil ? The young boy does not like to kill, but he is taught by the priest to carry out the will of an imaginary god. The boy is asked the indecent question "who made you," and the answer is forced on him, and he says, "God made me in his own image and his own likeness. The unsymmetrical shape of the body of the negro, if the answer is true, is the model of god. The Negro boy repeating the answer of the Christian catechism, if he is an intelligent boy, ought to feel that his god who created him is of the same shape as himself. An American boy when learning his catechism was repeating the words "god made me in his own image and in his own likeness," and the boy's little brother echoed : it is a bad model.

Teachers and parents who teach little boys to repeat foolishly what was taught to a nomadic tribe in the desert of Sinai in a barbaric age, do immense harm to the undeveloped child. Unscientific dogmas when diffused bring unhappiness to the world. Why should the little boy born in a civilized family, in an enlightened age be taught religious dogmas which were good for tribes when they were yet in the nomadic state, and when the scientific spirit had not yet been evolved ?

Children should be taught the ethics of the happy home. The law courts are full of cases wherein people are accused of theft, adultery, forgery, assault, defamation, drunkenness, selling opium or liquor without a license, cruelty to animals and so on, but no one is accused of the crime of atheism or nihilism. Punishments are awarded to those found guilty of having committed immoral deeds. It is therefore necessary to teach the child from his infancy that it is bad to be cruel, to steal, to fight, to tell lies, to drink intoxicants, to speak harshly, to back bite. This world of ours can be made happy if people would only abstain from committing immoral deeds. Muddleheaded priests and prophets wishing to dupe and dominate unmanageable tribes invented gods of cruelty, and taught the people that they will be punished if the god was not given the blood of bleating kids and innocent kine. To propitiate the imaginary gods created by pagan prophets millions of useful animals are slaughtered year by year, and the world is deluged by their blood.

Ask the child whether it is good to kill animals. and, if he had not been taught the metaphysics of speculative theism, he would most assuredly answer in the negative. He will say that stealing is bad, that associating with bad women is not good, that telling lies is bad, that backbiting is bad, that using harsh and abusive language is bad, that drinking intoxicating liquor is bad, and if he is asked why drinking liquor is bad, he will tell you that the drunkard loses his senses, that he beats his wife, and mother and father, and that he behaves badly. What is therefore needed ? Every child should be taught the ethics of the happy home, and the illiterate grown ups should be taught morality.

Child psychology is an interesting subject of study. Books teaching the cruel deeds of savage gods, and the inhuman immoralities of prophets and priests should be made taboo. Stories of heroes who had done noble deeds of selfsacrifice and charity should be taught to children. Stories of fathers who were ready to sacrifice their sons and daughters, and of brutal prophets who sent bears to tear up little children, and of saviours who cursed trees, and killed hogs by the thousands to please a mad devil, and of myths of creators who made man from his mouth and the dust of the ground, should be excluded from the kindergarten and the school. The immoral stories that the child hears influence him to repeat them and the innocent mind is poisoned and its growth towards truth is thereby arrested. Books containing immoral stories of gods and prophets and heroes should be excluded from the child's library. Destructiveness comes from an immoral, savage brain, and the good man can only teach to show loving kindness to all. Pride of birth and caste and colour has been productive of great unhappiness. The Ethics of Embryology and of Child Psychology may be taught

83

to all children in common from their 7th year. Truthfulness should be emphasised as a necessity in the life of the child. Truthfulness is immortal speech said the Blessed One. Learn to hear only that which is productive of kindness, truthfulness and selfsacrifice. Pride and Egoism are ignoble, and should be always condemned. The merciful Lord, the Blessed One, taught the Ethics of the Happy Home. May civilized humanity teach them to their children.

———

HOW THOUGHTS ARE GENERATED AND HOW THEY ARE TO BE CONTROLLED.

Religions founded upon priestcraft and dogma make man a slave of a despotic deity. Sankara says in his Commentary to the Vedanta Sutras that Isvara created the world and man for his own pleasure. The Creator is compared to a despotic prince who does whatever he likes. There is none to question him. The Commentator to explain the position of the despotism of the creator had recourse to an earthly illustration. The muddle headed people, illiterate and lacking the reasoning powers reconciled to the statement, and accepted the statement as a dogma. Machiavelli too based his arguments in enunciating his views on diplomacy seeing the despotism of Borgia.

Imagination of man is responsible for many things. Moses after having murdered an Egyptian escaped to Arabia and at Mt. Horeb met Jehovah. The result of the interview was the establishment of a religion. Mahammad fled from Mecca to Medina and having gained the support of the Bedouins of Medina succeeded in founding a religion.

Jesus with his little flock of disciples preached a

THE ARYA DHARMA OF GAUTAMA, THE BUDDHA.

doctrine which spread after his death rapidly in many
lands. Judaism, Islam of Mahammad and Christianity
are Semitic religions. The credulity of the human
mind is remarkable. A mere sound is enough to
change the views of a human being. Fasting and
prayer had been always popular with religious
minded people, and a moderate course of asceticism
and a well disciplined mind with a desire to live the
purified life help man to gain mystic insight into the
penetralia of mysteries.

There are dogmatic religions which show no
mercy to the fallen. Man lives on this earth for say a
hundred years, and then dies. There is no man while
he is yet alive, who refrains from doing a little good.
According to the dogma of a certain animistic religion
a man may have done good but if he does not believe
the dogma that a human being born some centuries
ago in some part of the Asiatic world, was the son of a
god, there is no salvation for him. Eternal damnation
in a hell is the punishment meted out to him. Men
who formulated such dogmas and founded religions
had no comprehension of the psychological nature of
the human mind. They never realized that man was
born with a purpose. Instead of promoting the happiness of humanity certain religious founders brought

more unhappiness to the world by their revolting dogmas.

For nearly fifteen centuries many millions of human beings have been tortured, oppressed, burnt, hanged, quartered for holding certain religious views that were not in conformity with the unscientific dogmas of the established religion. Millions of human beings have suffered death in vain on account of the devilishness of religious agitators. This earth which could be made the scene of human happiness, is converted into a slaughter house. Destruction without the agency of man there is enough on this earth. Cyclones, famines, plagues, tornadoes. earthquakes, tidal waves, &c., carry hundreds of thousands off to death. Man instead of lessening the death rate adopt the most diabolical methods to accentuate slaughter. Persecutions and destruction in the battle field are caused by human selfishness. If each one does what little good he can instead of committing evil, this earth would indeed be a happy place. Science and wisdom are brought into use to cause more destruction. The great war that is now being fought in Europe is devastating countries and millions are being sacrificed unnecessarily. The world is large enough for all but the covetousness of some is greater than others, and to this cause the great war is due.

Religion is a thing of the heart, and it is beyond the power of man to go into the heart of other people. To oppress a human being for his inner convictions is diabolical. Bruno was burnt at the stake by the muddle headed, ignorant ecclesiastics of Rome, and to-day we know that Bruno was right and the Vatican wrong,

Man is a thinking being, and he is changing every second in body and mind. He is not the same in thought for two consecutive minutes. The child of to-day who is ignorant of higher mathematics after he enters the higher form in the college may know to solve deep problems. To persecute a human being for religion is most inhuman. But the dogmatists, who adopted methods of persecution, had no knowledge of psychology, and of the psychical changes taking places in the human mind. Psychology was never a part of animistic religion. Dogma and psychology never go together. A religion without psychology is unfit for the thinker.

The only religion with a complete psychology. from beginning to end is the Arya Dharma enunciated by the Lord of Mercy, Sakya Muni, the Tathāgata Buddha. In renunciation the Blessed One found freedom from pride, selfishness and anger, and love came to live on earth, and the earth was happy, for the

bloody religions had not yet been born. Fair Aryavarta
was then purely Aryan, and the religion of love taught
freedom to man by psychological methods. Men and
women learnt the science, and they did not want
priests, gods, and animal sacrifice to realize emancipation from passion, anger, and ignorance. What was
wanted was effort and uprightness, and freedom from
hypocrisy. The desire to gain the higher wisdom was
developed, and the low desires for selfish gain were
by effort annihilated. This Wonderful Doctrine
perished from the land of its birth with the degeneration of the people who neglected the teachings of
wisdom and love. The generation that lived when the
final disappearance came were given to luxury and
sensual indulgence. Two thousand years of prosperity
made the later generations of the people to become
indolent and luxurious. Laziness and luxury were
responsible for the decline of the people of India.

Aryan psychology as enunciated by the Blessed
One analysed the human mind and classified the feelings, perceptions and volitions thereof into categories
of Good and Evil. To the Good belonged the meritorious thought, and to the evil the demeritorious
thoughts. Man was taught that in his hands lay his
own salvation, and that he is a responsible rational
being, and that by controlling his senses, evil thoughts

shall not arise, and that it is within his power to live a
life of perfect holiness here.

By the diffusion of the Doctrine of Love, brother-
liness was established, animals received kindness at
the hands of man, animal sacrifices ceased ; and
wisdom reigned. Psychological contentment is
spiritual wealth.

The Abhidhamma teaches that there are seven
mental phases to every act of consciousness : they are
first, (phasso, vedanā, saññā, cetanā, ekaggatā, jivitin-
driya, manasikāra.) contact, feeling, perception, volition, focussing, life energy and rational activity.

Second. Six mental conditions, viz., (vitakka,
vicāra, adhimokkha, viriya, pīti, chanda.) birth of an
idea ; investigation ; decision ; effect ; cheerfulness ;
lofty desire.

Third. There are fourteen mental phases which
are immoral, viz., muddleheadedness ; shamelessness ;
absence of fear to commit evil ; restlessness ; false
views ; pride ; ill will ; envy ; miserliness ; fretfulness ;
sleepiness ; dulness ; doubting. (moha, ahirika, ano-
tappa, uddhacca, lobha, diṭṭhi, māna, dosa, issā,
macchariya, kukucca, thina, middha, vioikicchā).

Fourth. There are nineteen mental conditions
which are ethically moral, viz., intelligent faith ;
recollectedness ; sense of shame ; fear of sin ;

generosity, non-hatred ; mental equilibruim ; mental
serenity : and bodily serenity ; lightness of body ; and
lightness of mind ; gentleness in feelings ; gentleness
of mind ; bodily activity : mental activity ; proficiency
in body and proficiency in mind ; uprightness of feelings and uprightness of mind.

Fifth. Right speech, right activity in abstaining
from killing, stealing and sensual indulgence ; and
right livelihood in abstaining from selling poisons,
liquor that intoxicates, weapons of destruction, flesh of
animals, and human beings.

Sixth. The two infinites, viz., kindness ; delightful
satisfaction.

Seventh. Analytical wisdom (paññā).

Things that we see, the sounds that we hear, the
smells that we inhale, the varieties of eatables that we,
taste, the objects that come in contact with our touch,
all have the characteristic of creativeness. The eye
meets with a form and the two coalescing produces the
eye consciousness, and the three coming together
produces contact ; contact—produces feeling, and
feelings produce thought germs which are called
samkhāras. Man is a creative being. Whenever the
sense organs are active a thought is in the process of
coming to existence. Some individual thoughts are
born and pass away without generating karma.

91

Others produce karma after having gone through the manifold processes which are called (patisandhi bhavanga, āvajjana, dassana, savana, ghāyana, sāyana, phusana, sampaticchana, santirana, votthappana, Javana, tadālambana, cuti) rebirth, continued existence, inclination, seeing, hearing, smelling, tasting, touching, receiving, investigating, determining, revolving, registering, ceasing to be. Before an impression is individualised it has to go through the different stages of psychological evolution.

We are living in a world of sense impressions. Every object however small is liable to create a thought, the minutest sound, the feeblest smell, the slightest taste, the least touch, or the former recollections of any one of these is sufficient to give rise to a thought. Ceasing to be and coming into existence, such is the ever revolving nature of the mind. It is compared to a monkey that is always busy, leaving one branch, catching hold of another, leaving that and getting hold of another. Every time an object is brought before the eye, the eye consciousness is produced, and then the evolution of the eye consciousness begins after receiving the picture impression in the mind. It investigates, determines and in the javana state the apperceptioning takes place. In the javana revolution before the final registering is done

92

the opportunity is given to abandon the object or to receive it is one's inheritance. If in the javana state the mind is inclined to the object, and the coalition takes place with either one of the elements of (lobha) covetous desire (dosa) anger or (moha) foolish imagination, the *karma* is formed. Within the twinkling of the eye through the sense organs the karma thoughts come into being. By controlling the sense organs and by a little practise of the evolving nature of each thought, an evil thought, before it becomes a fully developed karma, can be rooted out.

Hints to train the mind, to discipline the sense organs, to prevent new evil karma arising, &c., are given in the Abhidhamma sangaha. The Pāli copy cost only a few pence, with the commentary the volume cost about a rupee and a half. The English translation by Shwe Zan Aung, edited by Mrs. Rhys Davids may be had at the Oxford University Press, Bombay.

93

KARMA ACTIVITY AND ITS FRUITS.

Kamma or (Karma) is deed, and vipāka is the fruit. The field of activity is called karma kshetra. The thoughts or Viññāna are called (bija) germinating seeds.

The living being is composed of the five skhandhas, which are rupa, vedanā sañña, samkhāra and viññāna. Rupa is the physical body composed of the four great changing elements, viz., pathavi ; āpo, tejo and vāyo, which may be called the hard, or solid ; watery or liquid ; fiery or heat ; and the windy element or air. The physical organism when analysed may be divided into these four constantly changing elements. They are called the "mahā-bhuta" or the upādi rupa.

The development of the human cell in the womb of the mother is a subject of scientific study to understand the evolution of the embryo. Embryology, geology and biology are subjects that a student of the Abhidharma should study to know something of the evolution of the kalala bija (germinal seed) in the mother's womb. From the moment of the entrance of the seed into the womb it begins to go through the manifold processes of embryological evolution for nearly ten months, if in the interval no catastrophe falls to destroy the embryo.

In the ancient days in Egypt before its grand civilization was ultimately destroyed by the early Christians, the ancient Egyptians were taught that the deity formed man out of the earth. In the work called the "Dawn of Civilization" by Professor Flinders Petrie is given an illustration showing the formation of man by the deity from the earth.

If only people were taught the manifold processes of the evolution of the embryo, each one would then think that he began his career in the protoplasmic stage, that he first entered the tabernacle as a spirit and lived in darkness for nearly 300 days in the womb of his mother, like the deity who brought the Jews out of Egypt who lived in darkness for some four hundred years. There is no transmigration of a separate atman or soul in the animistic sense in the psychology of Buddha. There is the skhandha paramparā and the chitta paramparā without a break in continuity according to the law of cause and effect. Man is materialized karma, and karma are the thoughts generated in consciousness. Karma generated by evil thoughts are called demeritorious karma producing sorrow ; karma generated by pleasant thoughts

95

are called meritorious karma productive of happiness. Every ideation is a potential karma. Covetousness, anger, and unscientific comprehension of Dharma produce evil karma. Loving kindness, non-anger and scientific comprehension of Dharma produce good karma. Sankhāras ard the realm of fruition are interdependent. Every sankhāra has its sympathetic realm either in the kāmaloka or rupaloka or arupaloka.

To give a concrete instance : the eye sees, the eye consciousness takes cognizance of the form, and then goes through the stages of reception, deciding, fixing and the final impression is made after the fourth revolution of the fixing thought is associated with lobha, dosa, and moha, or alobha, adosa and amoha. Man is born of karma ; his own karma are his relations, his karma is his refuge ; he is the inheritor of his own karma. No god, creator, priest, brahman or king can interfere with his karma. Good karma elevates man, and his thinking power is purified and strengthened. Resoluteness to achieve great things has to be cultivated. The welfare of the world should be the impelling force to achieve great things. Compassion must always follow resoluteness. Every evil thought is reborn if not destroyed ; so does also a good thought. The karma generated in the past may all be destroyed by the accummulation of good karma. By the superabundant accumulation of good karma by strenuousness in this one life can emancipation be purchased. This is the secret that Buddha discovered under the Bodhi Tree.

Who created the skhandhas ? such a question is out of place in the psychology of the Abhidharma. There is no creation but growth. When the lady in Uncle Tom's Cabin asked the Negro girl Topsy, "who created you ?" she answered "I growed, nobody created me." The Rupa skhandha is undergoing changes momentarily, For two consecutive seconds there is no identity of even a particle of matter, but only continuity without a break. Man is therefore a highly complex compound, psycho-physiological in nature, undergoing changes with electronic rapidity, influenced by environments, of cold, heat, and feelings associated with pleasure, non-pleasure, and indifference, influenced by perceptions and appercentions, by means of objective pictures, forms, living and artificial, objective and subjective, creating karma with every volition, and consciousness taking cognizance of the whole phenomena "within this one fathom long body." Man is a creative being. He imagines things and gives life to them. According to the capacity of his own imagination he creates, and the phantoms that he creates become the bases of metaphysical superstructure.

In primitive society man is like a child willing to believe and to accept what he has heard, and that which is put before him in a persistent form he willingly accepts. Religions founded on metaphysical speculations belong to the region of myths. An ascetic constitution given to prayer and fasts becomes a prey to objective hallucinations. Take the case of Paul, who was on his way to Damascus, in the middle of the day, is attacked by a sun stroke, and falls on the ground. He had a guilty conscience and he came to the conclusion that it was God who had punished him for his persecuting spirit, and he forthwith accepts the principles of the religion that he had been trying to destroy. He never saw Christ in fiesh, although he was at Jerusalem, and it is the sound which he had heard that made him to express his compunction. On a mere phantom the whole superstructure of religion was built by the tent maker of Tarsus, and for nearly nineteen hundred years several hundred millions of people have been following the principles enunciated by Paul. In those days analytical science had not been born, and the illiterate people were easily duped to accept whatever was presented to them if only it could be shown that it was abnormal.

Nothing is more easy than to form a new religion provided the man who wished to impose his views on others had the wilfulness to become a charlatan. He must lose his sense of shame, and be willing to sacrifice his life. He should follow the path of the ascetic, and practise austerities in the way of fasting and live in solitude in some mountain fastness engaged in prayer. Asceticism is an essential requisite. Fasting and prayer and living in a mountain fastness have been a sine qua non with all religious promulgators. Moses was forty days and forty nights without food and drink in the mountain of Sinai. Jesus was engaged in fasting and prayer, and he especially recommended them to his disciples. Mahammad before he preached the religion of Islam was given to much fasting and prayer. He was praying to the gods of Mecca, and Allah heard him, and Mahammad was satisfied that Allah was speaking to him. Each individual according to the Aryan theory has an ishta devatā. Mahammad founded in Allah his ista devatā, and Allah became the central figure of his new religion. Jesus too prayed and fasted for forty days and forty nights and he found his ishta devatā in the heavenly father. Socrates had his ishta devatā and he was guided by the inner voice.

The Prince Siddhartha too heard the voice of Māra, chief of the celestial region, who promised all things on earth if he would give up his quest. The Prince was not satisfied with the material and divine pleasures of the lower and the higher heavens. The voice of Māra, was kind of will-o-the wisp, but he did not follow it. The greater gods appeared before Him, and when they found that His quest was different from all other people they worshipped Him. Religions that do not teach the doctrine of Kamma may be called micchādiṭṭhi. Certain religions do not teach a past but teach a future, and those that ignore the teaching of kamma may be called nihilistic. They teach a beginning a few thousand years back and an endless future either in a pleasurable or unpleasurable state. Any religion that ignores the doctrine of cause and effect is unfit for the thoughtful. The principles of Kamma and vipāka taken together postulate the scientific theory of the Conservation of Energy. Man is like an electric dynamo generating energy (Karma) every second. The mind is like the cinema machine.

Kamma paccayo and vipāka paccayo are two of the twenty four paccayas which form the basis of the seventh book of the Abhidhamma called the Patthāna. The Patthāna doctrine shows the cosmic process in its entirety, and the fulness thereof can only be appreciated by superior beings as the Buddhas and the Arhats. The twenty four pachchayas are Hetu ; ārammana ; adhipati ; anantara ; samanantara ; Sahā-jāta ; aññamañña ; nissaya ; upanissaya ; purejāta ; pacchājāta ; āsevana ; kamma ; vipāka ; āhāra; indriya; jhāna ; magga ; sampayutta ; vippayutta ; atthi ; natthi ; vigata ; avigata.

The Doctrine of Karma has been distorted by those who have not comprehended the subject in its entirety. The Blessed One enunciated the doctrine from the scientific standpoint and psychologically explained it to His Bhikkhus. The Karma doctrine was known to the Jatila ascetics of the Upanishad school who kept the sacred fire and these only were admitted to the Bhikkhu Order by the Blessed One without letting them go through the four months' probation (parivāsa). The members of the Sakya family were also exempted from the rule laid down about the parivāsa.

The members of Sakya family were exempted from the probation rule because they were related to the Blessed One, and the Jatila ascetics who kept the sacred fire because they accepted the law of Karma.

In the Chandogya Upanishad, Yajnavalkya is asked to explain the doctrine of karma, which he does in secrecy, thereby showing that it was an esoteric doctrine explained only to the followers of the Upanishad. The fact is mentioned that Yajna valkya explained to Artabhāga in secret the doctrine of karma and nothing more is recorded.

It was left to the Blessed One to explain the important doctrine in its fullness to His Bhikkhus and the lay followers.

Subha the young Brahman, son of Todeyya chief of the Todeyya school, one day came to the Blessed One and asked Him what is the cause that one man is born poor, another rich, one of low birth another high ; and the Blessed One explained that it is due to their karma.

The karma kānda of the Brahmans did not give the rationale of the psvchological operation of the doctrine of karma. To them karma was sacrifice and observing the rituals according to the Veda. The exoteric rituals, ceremonies. sacrifices etc formed. karma to the Brahmans. They had no idea of the operations of the karmic law from the standpoint of yathābhutañāna, which was the discovery of the Blessed Tathāgata, after He had won the divine knowledge of looking into the past, and looking to the future, after death. By the science of pubbenivāsā-nusmriti the Blessed One obtained the divine knowledge to look back into the past births of the individual and also to the past history of the earth. He saw the cosmic destructions and the reconstructions of countless billions of solar systems ; and by the divine eye of dibbachakkhu, He saw the future of the living being, how death follows birth, according to the karma he has done during life. Good deeds produced good fruits which gave birth to happiness either on earth or in heaven ; bad deeds bring birth in a state of suffering on earth, or in a purgatory or in the animal kingdom.

The fire worshipping Jatila ascetics practised the Jhānas and abhijñā, and obtained iddhi, and they looked to the past for many kalpas, and promulgated the law of good and bad karma.

After the attainment of the divine knowledge of looking into the past and looking to the future, the Blessed One did not rest, but pushed on in search of further wisdom, and then the supreme knowledge came that shook the foundations of the earth and heavens. The secret of life was revealed for the first time, and the Blessed One discovered the great Law of a Continuous Dependent Causality. Imasmim sati

103

idam hoti imassa uppādā idam uppajjati, yadidam avijjā paccayā &c.

A creative beginning was found to be baseless ; and equally false was the belief that life ends in annihilation. The law of change in its fullness the Blessed One comprehended, and the knowledge based on wisdom came to Him that nothing is permanent and nothing is annihilated, but only change in continuity. The error of the Egoists was that they took it for granted that things are permanent, and that a deity created matter out of nothing, at a certain period in the past. Fatalists formulated the erroneous idea that everything is predestinated, and that there is no need to make an effort to change the course of affairs. With a beginning in the past and an ending at death cannot but give rise to the error of nihilism. The ethic of nihilism was hedonistic enjoyments which gave rise to the saying "let us eat, drink and be merry for tomorrow we die." The ethic of Fatalism gave birth to the error of bodily mortification. Fatalism when associated with the idea of a deity creating the world is destructive to self and the world. The belief that a deity created the world several thousand years ago makes the muddle headed individual to invent a code of ritualistic practices to propitiate the deity by offering bloody sacrifices.

KARMA ACTIVITY & ITS FRUITS.

At the time when the Blessed One began to promulgate the Great Law of Dependent Causality with its corollary the doctrine of karma, India had accepted the broad principles of ritualistic practices called the karma kanda which made the followers of the Brahmans to give bloody offerings to the deity. Fatalism made the followers of the doctrine to adopt the ascetic life in its fullness, subjecting the body to extreme pain. Those who neither followed a deity nor adopted the ethic of the fatalist took to the nihilistic ethic of sensual enjoyments. Priestcraft naturally operates in full force when people are believers of the creative doctrine by a deity. With the deity is born the devil, and the poor people to escape from the devil, have to propitiate the god, and the priest rule then begins. Darkness appears with priest rule, because the devil is given a permanent place to torture the people. The priest gains his livelihood easily.

Nothing is permanent, nothing is annihilated, there is a continuity in the working of the Law of cause and effect in the change from eternity to eternity. Misery and happiness, profit and loss, praise and blame, prosperity and adversity, these are the links in the long chain of cause and effect. There is no creation and no annihilation, but only change.

Everywhere we see only motion and activity The atom is breaking to electrons and all life seem to follow a kaleidoscopic activity with the continuous productiveness of a cinema. Activity is the law of life. Karma and Vipāka follow each other as night follows day. The wise man comprehending this great law avoids evil, does good and makes the effort to purify the heart and live in peace with all, sending forth love to both god and devil, man and animal, and shows that he is grateful even to the shady tree that gave him shade.

DESIRE IN BUDDHISM.

Superficial students of the religion of the Lord Buddha, especially the followers of dogmatic beliefs, find fault with the teachings thereof that they destroy desire, and that a religion that destroys lofty desires is a pessimism, and that European races shall never accept such a religion.

Unfortunately for the cause of Truth no attempt has been made to show the hollowness of such a baseless assertion, and the Bhikkhus, have not done their duty to proclaim what the Blessed One taught. The three hundred millions of European peoples were satisfied with the Semitic religion of Canaan, and did not wish for more light. The Buddhist Bhikkhus and the more intelligent lay Buddhists have no idea of the conditions prevalent in Europe. For nearly fifteen centuries the European nations lived isolated, and when they woke up from their long sleep it was not to preach culture or religion that they crossed the oceans, but as apostles of the God of Mammon.

"A rabid race fanatically bold,
And steeled to cruelty by lust of gold

107

Traversed the waves, the unknown world explored ;
The cross their standard, but their faith the sword ;
Their steps were graves ; over prostrate realms they trod
They worshipped Mammon while they vowed to God."

Study of religion and the inquiry into the philosophies of ancient India began after the Upanishads had
been translated into Latin, and the first philosophical
thinker who investigated the Upanishads was the
German philosopher Schopenhauer. He had read of
the sublime life of the Buddha and found in the
philosophy enunciated by the Great Teacher a
resemblance to his own philosophy which was
generally known as a philosophy of pessimism.
Schopenhauer proclaimed his philosophy, and his
sympathy with Buddhism made the European students
of philosophy to label Buddhism as a pessimism.
Schopenhauer was more a student of the philosophy
of the Upanishads, nevertheless his sympathy with
Buddhism was enough for the common man to
denounce Buddhism as a pessimism. It proclaimed
the four noble Truths, and the first Truth was Sorrow,
and a religion that proclaimed sorrow as its first
principle was not the religion for the materialistic
European. He was frightened to think of sorrow, and
like the ancient gods who trembled when they heard
for the first time from the Blessed One the doctrine

108

of Transciency, (anicca) the dogmatists, theologians and hedonists shouted, "away with Buddhism we don't want it, it is a pessimism. and a religion that killed all desires. The pleasures of life, the high hopes were not to be given up, and a religion that killed all desires may be good to the people of India, but not to the virile European." Since the time of Schopenhauer the baseless assertion is repeated to the great detriment of philosophical enquiry.

Let us make a serious inquiry whether the Great Teacher did actually teach such a gospel to the world. Remember India is a continent, not like Palestine or Arabia, peopled by wild, roving Semitic Bedouins, children of the desert, and that it is a vast country peopled by highly spiritualized races, with a civilization going back to thousands and thousands of years, and the cradle land of religion and philosophies. In a country where religious inquiry is man's birth right, dogmatism has no place. India never knew in its long record of history to persecute people for their religious opinions. The persecuting spirit of religious tyranny began wiih the Semitic Jahvahism, and later ruthlessly followed by the founder of Islam. The Semitic spirit was implanted in the Latin and Teuton heart after the introduction of the Semitic doctrine of Palestine into Europe. Never having had a religion with a history and a theology the European races, it was quite easy for the promulgators of the Semitic faith to impress on the European mind the terribleness of the Jealous Jah of Mt. Horeb. Europe succumbed, and its future was made a blank by means of terrifying dogmatism ending with hell fire and brimstone to eternity.

Barthelemy St. Hilaire in France frightened the people of France by the pronouncement he had made that Buddhism is an annihilation. One hell fire was enough for the people, and if another was to proclaim annihilation, why the people will go mad !

In England the missionary was the sworn enemy of Buddhism. He proclaimed that it was a downright heathenism with devil worship as its complement. It was therefore fit for the cannibals, and the missionary actually proclaimed in his annual report that Buddhist parents did offer their children to crocodiles. With widow burning, infanticide, and the hideous Juggernaut car like the Moloch of the Old Testament demanding human holocausts, and worshipping stocks and stones, which the puritanic people of the British isles were asked to believe by the missionary, there was no hope for the acceptance of the Truth which the Great Teacher proclaimed to the Aryans of ancient India.

110

Recently a book was published under the title of "Trade, Politics and Christianity" by Longmans, Green & Co. Its author was one Mr. A. J. Macdonald, M.A., and the headhunter of Imperialistic politics, who knows all about the African hippotami and Rhinoceros and the Cannibals of Africa has contributed a glowing introduction thereto. This head hunter with the seriousness which make us blush says "Perhaps Pity as a cosmic force, was only born with the ministry of Christ." The history of the Inquisition, the slave trade in the hands of the British for nearly three centuries, the annihilation of the Tasmanians, the introduction of Opium into China at the point of the bayonet, the introduction of firewater into countries where no poisonous drinks were known before, the annihilation of the ancient people of Central America, the partial destruction of the Red Native races of North America, the lynching of helpless Negroes in the United States, the destruction of the feathered tribe for their beautiful plumage to adorn the heads of women, are all due to the birth of Pity in the hearts of the follower of Christ. The man has not read the Old Testament seriously and critically to find out what its contents are, and he has not seriously investigated into the dogmatics of Christianity with an eternal hell in flames, the rich man

111

being roasted for ever and ever with the loving father Abraham watching the operation with glee in the heavenly Elysium, singing hallelujahs !

"If you do not believe me I will send you to eternal damnation, where you will be continually roasted for ever and ever" : this is Pity in excelcis. And this Pity as a cosmic force was born with Christ nineteen centuries ago, and only began to show its power after the rise of imperialistic Christianity a century ago. The half civilized Spaniards and Portuguese in the sixteenth century had pity on the poor Aztecs and the rich natives of Asia. In order to save the soul of the Aztec and to rob his gold Cortez and Pizarro undertook voyages to Peru and Central America. In those days the Christian pirates and freebooters were simpleminded without the knowledge of Michiavellian diplomacy, and they did not talk and act as the modern political hypocrites do. The Spanish pirates were fanatics and they loved gold. Hypocrisy was not then a part of diplomacy. Cortez landed in Mexico and slaughtered the innocent Aztecs in 1514 ; the principles advocated by Machiavelli began to be studied long after. Machiavelli advocated "despotism sustained by cunning, unrestrained by morals". and modern political science is built on the foundations of this most brutal ethics. Despotism, Cunning and Immorality how could these non-human principles be associated with the divine quality of Pity ?

The Desire of the imperialist is world conquest. Pity has no place in his programme.

Does the Doctrine of Buddha kill desire ? The Buddha gave the answer in the Sankhāruppatti sutta in the Majjhima Nikāya, and in the Nidhikanda sutta in the Sutta Nipāta. It is the lofty desire associated with Pity that prompts the Bodhisat to abandon the eternal bliss of Nirvāna and plunge into the whirlpool of Samsāra, and work for the salvation of all Life, from the meanest to the highest divine being, for four asankheyya kalpas, a period that is beyond human calculation, but may be measured by imagination when it is known that the Bodhisat who became the Gautama Buddha had to get the confirmation from twenty four Buddhas successively, from the Buddha Dipankara to the Buddha Kasyapa. Pity unutterable again prompted the Prince Bodhisat, Siddhartha, in his last birth to renounce his wife, his only son and the love of his parents, when he was only twenty-nine years old, and to engage in study and meditation for six years, in the forests of Magadha, to discover the path of salvation to save men and gods. It was desire for happiness that makes one to aspire to attain

H
113

to the state of a pratyeka Buddha ; it is desire to realize the highest happiness that prompts the Buddhist to become ăn Arhat and realize the highest wisdom ; it is desire that prompts the good man to aspire for imperial sovereignty of a Chakravarti ; it is desire that prompts the thinking Buddhist to do good deeds and give the merits to others. Meritorious desires prompted the great Buddhist King Asoka to send missionaries to the then civilized countries of Asia ; it was desire that prompted the righteous emperor to give his own son and daughter to the Buddha sāsana ; it was the noble desire to serve that prompted the Prince Mahinda and the Princess Sanghamittā to go to Ceylon to preach the Dhamma to the men and women of Ceylon 2222 years ago. It was desire that made the immortal Buddhaghosa to leave India and go to Ceylon and write the Pāli Commentaries.

Desire is of two kinds, the noble and the ignoble. Noble desires prompt man to do works of charity, they make men sober, enlightened and good ; ignoble desires make men to adopt the policy of Machiavelli, to distribute opium, intoxicating liquor, and introduce syphilis and create bastards, and murder helpless people for the sake of rubber, gold and land.

114

DESIRE IN BUDDHISM.

Buddhism condemns ignoble desires, and emphasises on the necessity of cultivating noble desires. Buddha condemned (Tanhā) craving and lustful desire (Chandarāga) ; and emphasised on the development of (Chanda iddhipāda) the will to develop lofty desires, and to create (puññābhi samkhāras) meritorious deeds words and thoughts. Tanhā and chandarāga are born of Ignorance ; chanda iddhipāda and puññābhi samkhāras are born of (Pragñā) Divine Wisdom.

All good deeds, good words, good thoughts proceed from the element of Noble Desires, the Nekhamma dhātu and the Nekhamma sankappo of the Aryan Noble Path enunciated by the Blessed One the Buddha Sakyamuni.

THE ANCIENT STORY OF GENESIS AS KNOWN TO THE PRIMITIVE ARYANS OF INDIA.

In the Aggañña sutta of the Digha nikāya, the Blessed One, the Buddha Sākya Muni, related the ancient story of the genesis of the world to the two young Brahmans, Vāsettha, and Bhāradvāja, who left their homes to join the Holy Brotherhood of the Bhikkhu Sangha.

It is an interesting story making all human beings equal, and that man's glory consists in the observance of ethical laws in accordance with Truth.

Caste has no place in the ideal Democracy of Truth. The Blessed One is the best and most illustrious exponent of the sublime idea.

The Sakyans, the most haughty of the Kshattriyas of ancient India, who claimed descent from Ikhsvaku, the first of kings of the Solar Dynasty, in the Aggañña Sutta, are represented as being under the government of king Pasenadi' of Kosala. They are shown in the sutta, as paying honour and homage to the king. If there is any truth in the caste theory the King of Kosala should demand respect from the Blessed One.

But the King is guided by the higher ideal of Truth, and therefore the Blessed One who is a Sakyaputra, receives homage and worship from the king, in as much as he knows that the Samaṇa Gautama the Tathāgata is above him in wisdom and in the purity of His character.

Another important point shown in the sutta is that the ancient Aryans had a primitive tradition that the earth was first inhabited by the radiant beings who came from the Abhassara Brahmaloka. They were not created by the Brahmā of the Brahmanical tradition. The Brahman tradition was invented by the Brahmans to uphold their claim to superiority over the Kshatriyas and the other two castes. The Buddha in relating the ancient story demolished the Brahmanical dogma of the superiority of one caste over another.

The Kshatriyas claimed descent from the Sun-god, and laughed at the tradition of the Brahmans. They claimed superiority over the Brahmans in as much as they ruled over all other castes. They rejected the claim of the Brahmans, who posited a creator, whom the Brahmans called the Father of the Brahmans, from whose mouth they issued ! The Blessed One told the young Brahmans that in making Brahmā's mouth the womb of the Brahmans, they

defamed the God, Besides it is not true to say that
they came from the mouth of Brahmā, while the
living Brahman women are seen giving birth to babes.
By proclaiming an untruth the Brahmans were simply
committing a demeritorious act.

The Aryan ethics enunciated by the Blessed
One are:—That good man should not destroy life.
Destruction is the work of the savage and the pagan.
The dishonest life should be avoided ; the adulterous
life is bad ; unlawful sensuality is forbidden ; taking
intoxicants is bad ; falsehood, slandering others,
harsh and unpleasant language, unprofitable conversation are to be avoided ; covetousness, hatred, illwill
and erroneous and non-scientific views should be
abandoned. The noble Aryan should avoid these
unsocial immoral ethics.

The Blessed One pointed out to the two young
Brahmans that there are bad men as well as good men
among the Kshatriyas. Similarly there are bad and
good among the Brahmans ; and also among the
Vaishyas and Sudras· The Kshatriya, if he is willing
may become good, as also the Sudra. Truth and
Righteousness demand that the noble life of virtue
should be respected.

The establishment of a spiritualized Democracy
based on Truth and Righteousness was what the

Blessed One aimed at. The whole of the Vinaya Pitaka contain rules to guide the Brotherhood of Democracy. Every one was admitted within its portals, excepting the soldier, the epileptic, the leper &c. In as much as the king was against the admission of the soldier into the Bhikkhu Sangha, the Buddha did uphold the king's authority. The soldier has to bring his order of release from the army, when seeking admission into the Sangha. The leper, the man suffering from asthma and epilepsy and other incurable diseases were not admitted into the Bhikkhu Sangha in accordance with the wishes of the people. The Bhikkhus were expected to be examples of virtue and they were to preach the Good Law to the people, and visit them in their homes. The Buddha was asked by Jivaka, the Physician, not to ordain incurables, and the Blessed One laid down the rule that those suffering from incurable diseases should not be ordained. The Bhikkhu Sangha was a spiritual army and they were expected to travel nine months in the year from country to country, village to village, preaching and exhorting the people. Those that were suffering from incurable diseases could not carry out the rules of an active strenuous life.

No distinction of caste was made in the Order. But physical health was a necessity to lead the

vigorous life. The following is a free translation of the
Aggañña sutta, (second portion) showing the genesis
story according to the primitive tradition of ancient
Aryans :—

There comes a time after a very long period when
this world goes into dissolution.

At the time when the process of disintegration is
taking place the life wave ceases, and living beings
transmigrate and are born in the ābhassara Brahmaloka, the heaven of the radiant Gods.

Those who are born there have no material body,
they eat no solid food, in joy they live, and their
spiritual bodies are radiant, emitting rays of glory, and
they require no other light. They travel through
space. In happiness they live for a long long period.

There comes a time after a very long long period,
when this world begins to re-evolve again, Slowly
the world begins to re-integrate, and cosmic activity
commences.

When this world is fit to be re-peopled, the beings
of the Radiant world cease to exist there and are born
here.

And the incarnated beings are mind born, self-
evolved ; they live a life of joyousness. Their
spiritual bodies are effulgent ; perfect in symmetry,
beautiful to look at.

In this state of blessedness they exist for a long long period.

The earth is yet in a liquid form, water preponderates. Darkness impenetrable alone exists.

The sun and moon remain hidden. They are not visible. The spiritual beings have no idea of the starry space. The stars are not visible.

There is no Night and no Day, and time hath not. They know not of the day and of the night, and of the seasons and of years.

The beautifully shaped beings live in joyous innocence.

Differentiations of sex they know not. Apperceptions of sex have no place in their consciousness. This is Man and this is Woman they knoweth not. This knowledge hath not yet come to them.

Under the common designation of living being (sattā) these glorified spiritual beings exist.

In this condition of no-sex they live for a very long period.

Slowly and gradually the watery form that covers the earth disappear, leaving a surface of milky cream, in colour like unto gold.

And from this creamy surface of the earth there began to rise a perfume of divine sweetness.

The creamy surface gave the taste of divine

ambrosia. It was like unto sweet honey comb bereft of larva.

Inhaling the sweet perfume, illuminated by the glory of their own spiritual effulgent bodies, they traversed the skies, and there arose in them a curious desire to know what this creamy honey like substance was.

And they to satisfy the desire took a little of the creamy earth at the tips of their fingers, and applied it to their tongues,

And instantaneously the tongue felt the sweet taste of the fragrant earth, and desire arose in them.

In this tasting of the sweet earth there arose a low desire in man.

When they began to eat the sweet earth the divine effulgence of their bodies disappeared.

When the effulgence of their bodies vanished they felt darkness all round, and fear came over them. And they all willed and cried "let there be light"; and they saw the light of the sun ;

And when the light of the sun disappeared, they were afraid, and they cried again and said "let there be light", and they saw the light of the moon. Both these lights appeared synchronously.

And they saw the stars and the constellations, and now they came to know of the Day and of the

Night. They came to know of the changes in the seasons and of the year.

For a very long period man continued to eat the sweet creamy earth, and the development of the earth continued on.

Some human beings began to lose the beautiful complexion of their bodies ; and the differentiation of colour arose.

And those that did not lose their complexion began to despise those that had lost their colour. And thereupon appeared in man Pride.

And when pride appeared in man the sweet fragrance of the earth was lost.

And when they witnessed that the earth had lost the sweetness, they assembled in one place, and they began to express their grief in uttering the words "Oh we have lost the sweetness, Oh we have lost the sweetness."

And man found that he had no more sweet earth to eat, and he then found a kind of fungi springing up from the earth.

And when the fungi appeared on the earth, the watery nature of the surface of the earth had entirely disappeared.

And the earth was dry ground, and for a long

time man lived, eating the fungi which sprouted from the ground.

And there was a second disappearance of colour, and the beauty of their complexion vanished.

And those that had lost their colour were despised by those whose colour was not lost.

With the continued increase of pride in man there disappeared also the self-evolving eatable fungi.

And man found in the place of the fungi, a kind of rice that grew on dry ground, and then began to eat this rice which was sweet scented.

With increased desire and pride and eating the rice of the hill paddy, there came signs of femininity, and masculinity.

And there came in both a desire and they continued gazing at each other in an unusual manner, and the woman began to look at the man, and the man began to look at the woman ;

And this mutual gazing brought forth in the heart of man and woman passion.

And this passion grew, and the desire came in them to have sexual intercourse, and the desire was fulfilled.

And this intercourse was held not in private, and when others saw the act, they threw at them earth mud, handful of ashes, and cowdung, and said how can a human being commit such an act on another human being ?

And as time went on they forgot the unrighteousness of the act, and to commit the act they began to build houses.

And there arose in some the feeling of laziness, and thought why should I bring rice twice daily. It is only giving me trouble. So saying he brought enough rice to last the whole day.

To the man who had the store of rice another man came, and said, friend let us go to bring rice, and the man who had the rice said I have enough, and I do not want to go again.

And the other man thought why should I not follow this man's example, so saying he also stored up for the day. Whereby man came to know the value of storing up. With the storing up there was a further deterioration in the sweetness of the rice

Then man began to hold assemblies and began saying, we have departed from righteousness. They began to talk of the fall from their angelic condition ; and now they said we must not be reckless but we must now economise.

And they began to say : this is my share, this is my share.

And one man keeping his own share in safety, went and took by stealth another man's share.

And the other men caught him and said thou hast done an improper act, and they exhorted him and said do no such thing again,

And he assented, and again went and did the same thing.

Then some of them advised him, some beat him with their fists.

And when men began to steal more and more they began to punish the culprit.

And with the increase of sinfulness and evil deeds they assembled again and said :—

Let us come together and elect a man, who will do the work of a judge, who will punish us when we do wrong, and rebuke us when we need it.

And they all went to a man who was most beautiful, good to look at, powerful, and said, Excellent being, lead us righteously and we shall give thee a share of our rice ; and he assented,

And the men came together and elected the man in public assembly, and he was called "the great Elect".

THE DHYANA YOGA IN THE RELIGION OF THE BUDDHA.

The higher Dharma intended for the Brahmachari is an absolute transcendentalism. The Bhikkhu has to lead the perfect life of the saint, he has to lead the exalted life of the Buddhas and the Arhats. He has to follow the rules of the Pāṭimokkha, control his sense organs, and keep himself aloof from the ordinary path of the worldly man. Walking, lying down, sitting, standing, talking, keeping silent, in every movement of his limb he has to be wide awake. He has to discipline himself according to the rules laid down in the vinaya. The yellow robe is his garment. By begging he has to obtain his meal, and no solid food should he take after the sun passes the meridian. In quiet places, in caves, and in places of solitude, under shady trees, where he can enjoy the bliss of solitude, the Brahmachari should sit erect and practise the yoga of Breath. Fixing his visual consciousness in the centre of the heart, or at the tip of the nose, he should quietly begin to inhale and exhale keeping his consciousness all the while on the inhalations and the exhalations of his breath. He must know when he is

breathing, and be conscious that the breath that he
inhaled was long or short, and the breath that he
exhaled was long or short. He must refrain from
thinking of sensual pleasures, and never wish to go
back to the pleasures of sexualism. Money making
in whatever form should not engage his mind. He
must think of gold and silver as if they were poisonous
serpents. Their very touch is injurious to the Bhikkhu.
Contentment should be his fixed principle. Covetousness he must avoid. Anger, passion, harbouring anger,
pride, the spirit of revenge, conceit, arrogance,
stubbornness, slothfulness, delay to do good acts,
holding wrong ideas of religion, accepting nihilistic
views, envy, avarice, malice, generating polluting
desires, &c., these have to be abandoned. They are
contaminations. Moderate in eating, avoiding all
kinds of intoxicating liquors and narcotics, avoiding
falsehood, harsh speech, slander, idle gossip, he has
to think of only doing meritorious deeds of the higher
realms.

If the Bhikkhu is too much troubled by lustful
thoughts he has to follow the ethics of the rāgacharita,
and avoid such food, seats, garments, associates, residences, that would engender thoughts of lustful
passion. If he is troubled by angry thoughts, and
feels hatred towards others, he has to associate with

companions who will guide him in the path of love. he has to meditate the bhāvanā of loving kindness to all living beings ; he should have seats soft, and pleasant ; and his vision should come in contact with things that would not engender anger or hate. Food must be soft sweet and delicious and not hard and bad. The bhikkhu who is muddleheaded should cultivate the yoga of breathing, and associate with those who will guide him in the path of wisdom.

There are forty different kinds of mental fixities which are called karmasthānas. The brahmachāri who is inclined towards the higher life, who wishes to realize the bliss of Nirvana, may take one of the karmasthānas and begin training his mind. It is a process of self discipline to keep the mind wandering from one object to another. To bring the mind into a radiant state of infiniteness is the object of the discipline of the Buddhas. They first inculcate abstinence from all evil which are called the twelve akusalas ; and thence forward sublimate the mind by doing meritorious karmas of the four planes leading to the goal of Nirvana. All meritorious karma have to be done to enjoy celestial happiness. Doing evil leadeth to hellish states, although not eternally. To bring the mind into a state of radiancy is the object of the dhyāna yoga. For details consult the great work called the Visuddhi Magga.

The human consciousness is called viññāna or citta, or mano. The mind that is not brought under discipline goes downwards. The contaminations that lead the mind to the lower grades of hellishness, animality, ignobleness, viciousness are called *kilesas*. What the kilesas are may be known by the simple word contamination. That which pollutes the mind has to be avoided. Every thought that is the result of anger is a contamination ; every word spoken in anger and hatred and malice is a contamination ; every word spoken with lustful feelings is a contamination ; every thought produced with lustful feeling is a contamination ; every deed done with a low desire and based on covetousness is a contamination. Every thing done in the spirit of self-sacrificing altruism is meritorious.

There are eighteen foolish questions about the ego which have to be avoided, relating to the present, past and future. Buddhism is not a nihilism ; nor is it an agnosticism. It is not a religion of dogmas. It is a religion of truths based on analysis. Every idea is subjected to analysis. It is not a monotheism and acknowledges no creator. It is not a nihilism in that it posits the law of causes and effects, with an eternal

future and an eternal past. It is not an egoism, nor
is it a pantheism. It avoids speculation. It is founded
on the Four Noble Truths. It accepts the beliefs of
the existence of gods, and great Brahmas, who are
chiefs of world systems. One great Brahmā can, by
his power, illuminate by his own glory ten thousand
world systems. The Buddhist hates neither god nor
devil. He has no quarrel with the religions of the
ante Buddhist period nor with religions of the post-
Buddhist period. He loves all ; he analyses every
dogma, rejects the bad accepts the good.

> Sabbapāssa akaranam
> Kusalassa upasampadā
> Sacitta pariyo dapanam
> Etam Buddhāna Sāsanam.

The Blessed One is the great Teacher and Guide
of both gods and men. Analysis of mind and
body ; spreading loving thoughts throughout the
universe ; resolute will to reach the goal by good
words, good deeds and good thoughts—this is
Buddhism.

SELECTIONS FROM PSALMS OF THE BRETHREN

(*Translated by Mrs. Rhys Davids.*)

My heart is well composed, my heart is free
And ardent is my mood, Now rain, Cloud ! rain

Subhuti.

Alone, content, in meditation ecstacy
Victorious, no more by creeping dread dismayed
He mindful watcheth over sense with courage high.

Sitavaniya.

All longings as to this or other life
Have I put far from me, as one who hath
Beta'en himself to truth, whose heart's at peace
Who, self subdued, in all things undefiled
Discerns the world's incessant ebb and flow

Punnamasa.

In wisdom strong, guided by virtue's rule,
To concentration's raptures given intent yet vigilant,
Partaking of such fare as brings thee only good
So in the faith, with passions quenched await the hour

Gavaccha.

SELECTIONS FROM PSALMS OF THE BRETHREN.

All unafraid of death, nor fain to live
I shall lay down this compound frame anon
With mind alert, with consciousness controlled.

Ajita.

Since sickness hath befallen me, O now
Let there arise in me true mindfulness
Sickness hath now befallen me—'tis time
For me no more to dally or delay.

Uttiya.

In the great forest, in the mighty woods,
Touched though I be by gadfly and by gnat
I yet would roam, like warrior elephant
In van of battle, mindful, vigilant

Gahvaratiriya.

E'en as she would be very good
Towards her only child, her well-beloved son
So too ye should be very glad
Towards all creatures everywhere and every one,

Sopāka.

O goodly are the things our ears now hear ;
O goodly is the life we here may lead !
O good it is always to lack a house !
Now questioning on things of high import
Now showing all due thanks and reverence :
Such is the calling of the true recluse
Of him who owneth naught of anything.

Kuma's Son.

133

THE ARYA DHARMA OF GAUTAMA, THE BUDDHA.

As one down smitten by impending sword
As one whose hair and turban are aflame
So let the Brethren mindful and alert
Go forth, all worldly passions left behind.

Tissa.

Go meditate, Sumangala, ay go
And meditate, Sumangala, and bide
Earnest and diligent, Sumangala

Sumangala.

Do nought of evil, open or concealed
If evil thou now doeth or wilt do
Thou'lt not escape from ill.

Sānu.

In trust and hope forth from my home I came
Into the homeless life and there is me
Have mindfulness and sight grown. and tense
And well composed my heart and mind
Make thou whatever shams thou list
    Thou'lt harm me not

Sāmiddhi.

Buddha the wake, the Hero hail ¡ all hail ¡
Thou who from every bond art wholly free !
Strong in the lore I learnt of thee, I live
From fourfold venom cleans'ed sane, immune.

Ujjaya.

134

The burdened earth is sprinkled by the rain
The winds blow cool, the lightnings roam on high
Eased and allayed the obsessions of the mind
And in my heart the spirit's mastery

Vimala.

The heart of me is steadfast and at peace
Now on it pleaseth thee to rain, cloud, rain

Godhika.

Deep in the leafy glades of Anjana
My couch into a little hut I made
The threefold Wisdom have I made my own
And all the Buddha's ordinance is done

Anjana Vaniya.

O godly is the sight of cultured minds !
Doubt is cut off and wisdom grows apace.
E'en of a fool they make an able man ;
Hence goodly is the intercourse with saints.

Susārada.

Where men are arrogant, see thou lie low
Where they are low in mind lift up the heart.
Dwell thou where other folk care not to dwell,
Wherein men find delight, take thou no joy.

Piyañjaya.

All passion have I put away, and all
Ill will for ever have I rooted out,
Illusion utterly has passed from me ;
Cool I am now.   Gone out all fire within.

Rakkhita.

All action wrought by me and bringing birth,
Whether't was of great potency or small,
Shattered and ended is it utterly.
Now is there no more coming back to be

Ugga.

Whatso of evil wrought in bygone days
In former births by me, just here and now,
Tis that whereby I lie and suffer sore—
But other ground for ill exists no more.

Samitigutat.

The holy lore and liberty quest,
All lurking vain conceits I cast away

Si'vali.

He who doth dwell on highest plane of thought,
With Zeal unfaltering, Sage, Arahant,
In wisdom's branches trained such as he is
No sorrows may beset him who with mind
Calm and serene and clear, abideth aye

Ekudāniya.

Only virtue here is highest ;
But the wise man is supreme
He who wisdom hath and virtue
He 'mong men and gods is victor

Punna.

Is there a man who can the truth discern
Tho' it be very subtle and refined
Who, skilled to measure spiritual growth,
Is yet of lowly and of gentle mind,
Who shapes his life by rule of Them that wake :
For him Nibbāna is not hard to find.

Vacchapāla.

With sensuous desires, with enmity
With sloth of mind and torpor of flesh
A brother hath no truck, and in his heart
Turmoil of any kind and doubt are dead

Suyāmana.

JENTA'S SOLILOQUY.

Infatuated with my birth, my wealth
And influence, with the beauty of my form
Intoxicated, thus I led my life.
O'er much I fancied none was like me
A poor young fool by overweening spoilt,
Stubborn with pride, posing and insolent.
Mother and father, ay and others too

Claiming respect and honour, never one
Did I salute, discourteous, stiff with pride

Jenta.

THE BLESSED ONE'S ADVICE TO JENTA.

For mother and for father too likewise
For eldest brother, for the teacher, for
The Brahman and for them of the yellow robe :
For these is one to cultivate no pride,
These should one honour, these should one revere,
To these if one show reverence it is well.
The Arhants cool, adept, sane immune,
For whom pride perished as they crossed the goal,
To them beyond all others homage pay.

DHAMMAPALA'S SONG.

The brother who while young hath given himself
Wholly to carry out the Buddha's plan
Who keepeth vigil in a sleeping world
Not vainly, not for naught he spend his days.
So let the wise man, so let him who aye
Remembereth that which Buddhas have enjoined,
Devote himself to faith and righteousness
To know the blessedness They brought to us
And the true vision of the holy Norm.

<hr>

138

EAST AND WEST

The Lord Buddha came to preach to the world of
gods and men the holy doctrine of Peace and contentment. When He appeared in the sacred soil of
Aryavarta, modern religions were unknown. Between
Asia and Europe communication there was not. The
Greeks and the Romans knew of the territory known
to-day under the name of "Asia Minor." The historic
and classic city of Troy was in Asia Minor, and the
city founded by Alexander the Great was in Egypt.
The Greeks fought with the Persians when Xerxes was
the King of Persia. Greece, Egypt, Babylonia,
Assyria, Persia and Asia Minor were seats of civilization several thousand years ago. The Minoan
civilization of Crete is about 8000 years old. The
ancient Egyptian civilization was neither Semitic nor
Negro. Egyptologists are of opinion that it is of
Asiatic origin. The extreme west of Asia Minor which
comprised the ancient countries of Mysia, Lydia and
Caria was known to the ancient Greeks as Asia.

In the sixth century B.C., Persia was highly
civilized. The ancient civilization of Greece was
Oriental in character. The ancient Greeks thought

like the ancient Aryans of India, the gods they worshipped were not of the semitic type. Zeus was the chief god of the Greeks, and in the classic age the Aryan god was Indra. In dress, in manners, between the ancient Greeks and the ancient Aryans of India there was much similarity. The draped figures of the Greek poets and philosophers were exact representations of the statues of ancient Aryan Bhikkhus. The modern Indian Sari and the cloak worn by the ancient Greek women were similar. The classical dress of ancient Rome was purely Aryan.

The religions of Persia, Egypt, Babylonia, and India helped the religious thought of Rome. The poets of Greece, and Rome before the latter country went under the domination of the Semitic religion, gave to the world their great thoughts in accordance with the spirit of harmony. The idea of an eternal hell came like a miasma poisoning the atmosphere of freedom. Despotism was enthroned and freedom of thought was no more possible.

The ancient Romans had a culture to give before the time of Constantine. With the birth of the new cult under Constantine the world trembled that a dark period of the world's history dawned. Under Imperial Rome there was religious freedom. Slaves like Epictetus gave the most sublime ethics to the Roman people. Marcus Aurelius was infinitely supreme to Constantine who murdered his own wife and son. Did he after his conversion become better ? Asoka before his conversion was inhuman ; but after his conversion to Buddhism he became humane.

The Roman philosophers were followers of the school of Pythagoras, and they also accepted the principles of the school of Stoics. The Egyptian cult of Isis had spread all over the Roman empire' Isis was the prototype of the Virgin cult. Mithra was the Sun god. Osiris was the prototype of the dying god. In imperial Rome students and philosophers of the different schools of religious thought met in harmony, and Rome adopted the law of religious neutrality. What made Rome decadent was the influx of slaves from all the conquered territories to the capital. Slaves were given freedom under certain conditions. The slaves accepted the teachings of Jesus since they suited the slave temperament. Such ethics as "My kingdom is not of the world ; Blessed are the poor ; blessed are they that are persecuted for my sake ; If thou will be perfect go and sell all that thou hast and give to the poor ;" were acceptable to the slave temperament.

The ancient Aryan Bhikkhus were great builders of civilization. The civilization of Greece and Asia

THE ARYA DHARMA OF GAUTAMA, THE BUDDHA.

met in harmony when the great Alexander crossed the
Hellespont and came as the conqueror to Persia
through Egypt. The ancient countries of Sogdiana,
Bactriana, Ariana, Gedrosia, Persia, Parthia, Media,
Babylonia, Syria up to the confines of Indus felt the
invader's power. Unfortunately the great Alexander
in his thirtieth year fell a prey to the pleasures of
Persia. The conqueror was conquered by the Evil
One. He died a victim to alcoholism. Thence-
forward between Greece and India there was a
continuous interchange of ideas. Alexandria became
the centre of learning. The followers of Zoroastrian-
ism, the Stoics, Neo-Platonists, the followers of the
school of Epicurus, the Cynics, and the Essenes met
at Alexandria and exchanged ideas on things
spiritual. The Essenes taught the principles of
Buddhism. In the article "Roman Asceticism" Mr.
J. S. Reid says :—

> "Platonism was early influenced by Stoicism,
> and the Neo-Platonic movement of the
> third and later centuries resumed and
> enforced the ascetic elements in the earlier
> systems······ But the most important
> movement of all was that great missionary
> movement which began early in the period
> of the empire. Philosophers, often Cynics,

but often also calling themselves by other names, left their studies and went forth into the streets of great cities and preached to the people, urging them to change their lives and to follow after purity and abstinence, and to listen to the Divine call."

—*Encyclopocdia of Ethics*, p. 109, Vol. II.

The early Pythagoreans, Platonists, the followers of Isis and Osiris ; of Mithra, the Persian Sun god ; the Stoics, whose best exponents were Marcus Aurelius and Epictetus ; the Neo-Platonists represented by Apollonius of Tyana, all helped to keep the torch of philosophy burning in the Roman empire. Amidst these philosophical surroundings the slaves of Rome and the Plebian class managed to hold worship in the catacombs secretly in honour of the Christ-god who was slain as a sacrifice. Without any specialized ethics, with no foundation of philosophy, the Semitic Cult built on the fears of hell and hopes of a future heaven, gained adherents. To the philosophical Greek virile in his ethic, the mystical emotionalism had no attraction. To comprehend the psychology of the situation it is very necessary for the student of religion to read Gibbon's' "Decline and Fall of the Roman Empire."

The ancient Hellenes had a king of spiritualized democracy in the age of Pericles. The ancient Buddhists of Ceylon cultivated wisdom, and they attempted to lead the perfect life. The island was admirably suited for the Arcadian life. The people of India had plenty, and they gave their civilization and culture to foreign nations. India civilized Japan, Burma, Siam, Tibet, Mongolia, Manchuria, China by giving the people of those lands a religion based on love and wisdom. The brigand was reformed, the lover of art had much to learn, agriculture was developed, and architecture received encouragement for further development. The ancient Indian Buddhist Bhikkhus made every effort to test truth by their self-sacrificing lives. They conquered lust, anger, and foolishness. They triumphed, They were patient, they started on great missions, confident that self-sacrificing efforts are not wasted, but help humanity like a refreshing shower of rain,

The world after a thousand years of the Buddha's parinirvana underwent change. Three great events happened simultaneously in Asia. In Middle Asia there was the glorified doctrine of the Buddha in full development ; in West Asia Muhammad killed all the gods and elevated Allah ; in the far East Buddhist Bhikkhus sowed the seeds of the Eternal Dhamma,

144

Synchronously with the consummation of the events,
the Semitic religion of the far west of Asia was
established in the extreme west of Europe. When we
read the history of ancient Greece and of Rome we
feel as if we are treading on Asiatic ground. A
degenerate ecclesiasticism arrested the growth of
Europe. Pythagoras, Empedocles, Homer, Euripides,
Sophocles, Aeschylus, Socrates, Heraclitus, Democri-
tus, Plato, Aristotle, certainly were superior to the
bigoted fanatics of the early Roman church. The
philosophers of Rome who had taught and preached
before the birth of Constantine were great. The
pre-Christian Romans were not barbarians. They
were virile and they wished to rule the world. A
Roman poet sang

"Others may beat the bronze as soft as flesh,
And mould the marble to the living face
    Plead causes better, pencil out the heavens,
    And tell the story of the rising stars.
To rule the world-that is thy mission Roman,
    Thy art is to lay down the law of peace"
    Sparing the conquered, trampling on the proud.

The ancient Buddhists too conquered, but in a
different way. They conquered by love, and they did
not trample on the proud, but by moral persuasion

J   145

showed the vileness of being proud and arrogant.
Without the sword in hand the Bhikkhus by the force
of Wisdom and mercy conquered the continent of
Asia.

THE COMMON LANGUAGE OF
ANCIENT INDIA

When the Blessed One, Lord Buddha began His mission of Love and Freedom the Gangetic Valley had one common language. The great University at Taxila was on the border province of Gandahar. The people of Gandahar were in touch with the people of the Gangetic valley. In the commentary of the Dhatuvibhanga sutta, Majjhima nikāya, is found the story of the young prince Pukkusāti who having renounced his principality came to Magadha in search of the Blessed One, and the Blessed One preached to him the discourse on the Analysis of Organic and Inorganic Elements. In the Commentary of the Vinaya Piṭake the story is given of the Gandahar merchants and traders coming over to the kingdom of Magadha and meeting King Bimbisāra, contemporary of the Blessed One. The King sent an epistle engraved on gold plates and written on silk cloth and enclosed in a lacquer box wrapped in costly silks to the King of Gandahar. It was written in Magadhi. In the commentary of the Mahapari Nibbāna Sutta, it is mentioned that the Vajjians had their laws written

147

in a book. It was called Pavenipotthaka. In Kosala
Magadhi was spoken. Gandahar was the seat of
learning, and there is evidence to show that at that
period both Sanskrit and Magadhi were spoken.
Salatur a city in Gandahar was the birth place of the
great Sanskrit Grammarian, Pānini, and the University
of Taxila was famous throughout India. There Greek
and Indian Aryan met and exchanged ideas. The
exchange of ideas ceased after the invasion of the
Cabul valley by the followers of Mahammad.

The Edicts of the great Emperor Asoka who lived
200 years after the Parinibbāna of the Buddha show
that he carried his victorious arms from sea to sea, and
the west extreme of his empire was at Taxila. East,
west, north, south, the good emperor carried his
gracious message of the Law of Righteousness by
means of his wonderful edicts, and also by his
ambassadors, and accentuated by the self-sacrificing
labours of the noble army of yellow robed Bhikkhus,
members of the Sangha of the Blessed One. There
was one common language used which was called
magadhi, the *lingua franca* of India. Naturally the
army of the yellow robed Bhikkhus went all over India
and founded schools and colleges with hundreds and
thousands of students who were taught Pāli, the
language of the Buddha. The Buddha did not wish

148

that the ornate language of Sanskrit should be used to
convey His message to the people. His mission was
to elevate the people, and the language of the
Brahmas being Sanskrit the people could not be
taught through that language, and the Blessed One
therefore insisted that the message of the Blessed One
should reach the people in their own dialect, that is
Magadhi, which the Buddha used ; and to suit the
subject it was necessary that the langurge should be
purified, and in the pnrified form it was known as
Pāli.

The edicts of Asoka are not in Sanskrit but in the
dialect of the province wherein each edict was
written.

In the extreme south of India in the island of
Ceylon where the Bhikkhus of Buddha had their
monasteries, Pāli and pure Magadhi were studied.
This is but natural. When the Arabs won their
victorious battles on foreign soil, they ordered their
language should be taught to the new converts.
Wherever a victorious nation goes their language is
taught to the people brought under subjection.

The progress of the Magadhi language, in India
was stopped after the invasion of India by the Arabs.

The inscription found on the Relic Box at
Piprawa, about twenty years ago, was in Magadhi,

THE ARYA DHARMA OF GAUTAMA, THE BUDDHA.

and Piprawa is in the Nepal valley. In Ceylon the
whole of the Three Pitakas was handed down from
generation to generation by word of mouth for nearly
two hundred years, and in the reign of Wattagāmini
Abhaya the three Pitakas were reduced to writing, a
hundred years before the birth of Christ. Happily for
the world this occured before the birth of Christianity.

The Pāli scholars of the West, especially in
Germany have been ransacking their brains to find out
the birth place of Pāli. Oldenburg is of opinion that
Pali had for its home the country south of the Vindhya
mountains. Another noted critic of Pāli is Dr. Franke.
Dr. Franke has not accepted Oldenburg's view. His
view is that the home of Pāli may be found between
the middle and western Vindhya mountains. There
is another critic Dr. Windisch. He differs in his con-
clusions with Franke and Oldenburg and says that the
Buddha used the language of Magadha.

These Oriental scholars are fighting for the husk.
The Blessed One wished that the language used to
convey the message of Buddha should be the language
of the people, and not Sanskrit. Why dogmatise and
mislead ignorant people in the West. Magadhi,
Suraseni, Paisachi, Maharashtri, Prākrit were the
dialects spoken by the people at the time, and the
Blessed One beautified the vernacular by inventing

expressions and terms to expound His wonderful Doctrine of the Bodhi pakkhiya Dhamma. Pāli may be called the middle language which was used by the Blessed One to expound the Doctrine of the Middle Path. The ornate and embellished Sanskrit and the vulgar Paisachi Prakrit, He avoided, and made a classic of purified Magadhi, which was called Pāli to designate the language that He used as different from existing dialects. Pāli is the language of the Buddha which could easily be understood by the natives of Magadha, Kosala, Sauraseni, Kasi, and Gandahar.

Sir George Grierson, at one time Collector of Gaya, the best linguist of Hindi dialects, has contributed an essay to the Memorial volume of Sir Ramkrishna Gopal Bhandarkar under the title "Home of Pāli". It has useful information which he has collected from various sources. Sten Konow in his article on the "Home of Paisāci" has shown the resemblances that exist between Pāli words and the Paisāci Prakrit. Dr. Grierson in his interesting Essay gives a list of the places where the Paisāci dialects were spoken. They are : Kancidesiya, Pandya Pañcāla, Gauda, Māgadha, Vracada, Dākshinātya, Saurasena, Kaikeya, Sabara, Dravida. This list is taken from Mārkandeya. Dr. Grierson following Lakshmidhara gives another list wherein Paisaci was spoken : viz., Pāndya, Kekaya, Bahlika, Simhala, Nepāla, Kuntala, Sudhesna, Bota, Gandhara, Haiva and Kannojana. Says Dr. Grierson,

"The first thing that strikes one about these three lists is the great extent of country that they cover. If we are to accept them in their entirety, Paisaci Prakrit was spoken over nearly the whole of India and also in Tibet."

Since the time of the Blessed One the Pāli language began spreading not only in India, but beyond which may be called, the Greater India. Wherever the Buddhist Bhikkhus went there arose centres of literary culture, and they transplanted Indian art, agriculture, gardening, floriculture, architecture, etc., and the countries which accepted the Message of Peace and Love looked to India as their motherland. For a thousand years India was the spiritual home of the nations beyond. Jave, Cambodia, Korea, Japan, Siam, Burma, Tibet, Gandahar, Bahlika, were Buddhist centres, and the scholars of these countries naturally had to study Pāli and other Prakrit dialects. Gandahar, Bahlika, Jave, and the countries to the west of Gandahar were brought under the dominion of Koran, and Aryan culture ceased. India is on more the home of Buddhism.

After a period of nearly seven hundred years the

study of Pāli has again been taken up by a number of students in the University of Calcutta. The Maha Bodhi Society published the first Pāli Grammar in the month of October 1901, edited by Dr. Satis Chandra Vidyābhusana of the Calcutta University. Since then a little has been done to encourage Pāli studies in Bengal and Maharashtra.

With the development of the vernaculars in India the time may come when Pāli would be studied. Without the illuminating doctrine of the Buddha India is engulfed in darkness. To elevate the people the study of their own vernaculars is most necessary, and when the vernaculars are encouraged, Pāli might be easily introduced, and through Pāli the millions will then again come to know of the redeeming love of the Blessed One.

Oh for a good Buddhist king to-day to held the diffusion of Buddha knowledge among the dumb millions of India. The few wealthy Buddhists of Japan, Siam, China, Burma could help the spread of Buddhism in India, but as they are of the Mongolian race India is to them a kind of forbidden land.

But a gleam of light is visible in the little community of Buddhists in Chittagong. Already a few young men have taken up Pāli. One of the young Chittagong Buddhists, Beni Madhav Barua, a graduate of the Calcutta University, has been awarded the degree of Doctor of Literature by the London University. The Buddhists of Chittagong speak Bengalee, and through Bengalee literature their progress is sure to come. But they are as a community not endowed with wealth. The Buddhists of Siam, Japan, Burma, Ceylon and China may help them; but in the heart of the modern Buddhist love is little visible. Selfishness has taken deep root in the modern Buddhist heart. But for the compassionateness of early Aryan Bhikkhus of India, the culture which the people of these countries enjoy could never have been possible.

We hope that the Buddhists of Asia will make every effort to foster the spirit of unselfish love, and help the diffusion of the sun light of Truth in non-Buddhist lands. The Buddhist Bhikkhus of ancient India imbued with the spirit of compassion and inspired by the teachings of the Blessed One went to various countries of Asia and preached the Dharma to non-Aryan races. We expect to see the forgotten spirit of Buddha's compassion revived in Buddhist countries.

painted woman in the most brilliant colours describing
her loveliness to an extravagant degree. The erotic
hymns in her praise, and the ascetics found in her the

WOMAN IN ANCIENT INDIA

Woman in ancient India was free. India is the
home of the spiritual ascetic and the devotee of
sensual pleasure. Works on Kāmasāstra written in
Sanskrit are an indication of the bacchanaliad orgies
which were current in ancient days The ascetic
worked up wrath against woman, for she was to him
the one obstacle to spiritual progress. The gods sent
celestial virgins to tempt the saint, and as he had
invariably succumbed, woman appeared to him as a
she demon, and the only way to success in the
spiritual path was to avoid her company.

The conflict arose between sensual pleasure and
the saintly life. Those who had triumphed in the
path found the happiness of the Brahmaloka gods,
which was above sensual pleasure. This led the
ascetics to persevere in the path of Yoga and Brahmachariya. The happiness of the lower heavens was
within the easy reach of the good househoder. The
good wife, chaste, active, attentive to household
duties, obedient, loving her husband and willing to
die for him was praised, and her reward for her
womanly qualities was birth in heaven. Indian poets

painted woman in the most brilliant colours describing
her loveliness to an extravagant degree. The erotic
literature was abundantly large. The poets sang
hymns in her praise, and the ascetics found in her the
embodiment of evil.

Indian woman lost her individuality after the
Moslem invasion of India. Woman was not considered sacred by the Semitic races. The story of Adam
and Eve had made woman degraded for ever. By
her was sin introduced to the world, and she must be
guarded to prevent her from doing more mischief.
The ancient Persians also it appears had their women
guarded anq veiled. The Arabian women before the
time of Mahammad it seems had the freedom to
choose her own husband. The story of Khadija
shows how business like she was in her dealings wiih
the young overseer, whom she took as her husband.
That Polygamy was current in Arabia and in
Mesopotamia we learn from the story of Abraham.
Sarah herself suggested to her husband to take the
servant woman Hagar. The Bibilical heroes of the
Old Testament were veteran polygamists.

India being almost a continent evidence shows
that the institutions of polygamy, polyandry and
monogamy had existed in the remotest times. The
Pāndava brothers had one wife in common. The

gods were monogamous. Indra, Shiva and Vishnu had each only one wife. The war god Kartika was a bachelor. It is said that when Brahmā was making the body of the woman that he shut his eyes lest he may fall. Shiva was tempted and came out triumphant at first, but again fell.

Indian Aryan women were always free. To-day she is free in the provinces of Bombay, Madras and other provinces where the Moslem influence did not penetrate. The Semitic story degrades woman, but in India the mother is worshipped. Bengal is specially devoted to the adoration of Durga and Kali. The Bengalee invokes the aid of the mother Kali. In the United Provinces and in places where Krishna and Rāmā are worshipped, their names are associated with that of their wives. The Earth is represented in the form of a Goddess. In the great conflict under the Bodhi Tree with Māra and his hosts the Blessed One called the Earth to w;tness that He was the conqueror.

When the Lord Buddha began His mission it was not to man alone that He proclaimed the Dharma. Previous to the time that He began to preach already women had left their homes to lead the life of the homeless. The Nirgrantas had their women ascetics. The Theri Gāthā a pāli work belonging to the

157

Khuddaka Nikāya, of the Sutta Pitaka, contains the poetical Gāthās composed by the Bhikkhunis who wore the yellow robe. It has been translated into English by Mrs. Rhys Davids under the title of "Psalms of the Sisters".

The Bhikkhunis were addressed as Sisters by the Bhikkhus. They were preachers and teachers, and some of the great Bhikkhunis belong to the highest families in Magadha. The wife of King Bimbisāra by name Khema, the most beautiful among women, became a Bhikkhuni seeing the changing nature of things. She was so beautiful that she nevar cared to visit the Blessed One, as she heard that the Buddha speaks against beauty. The Buddha one day went and sat in the royal garden, and the King wishing to take her to hear the doctrine of the Blessed One, without telling her of the Blessed One's visit, simply expressed his desire that she might accompany him to the pleasure garden. The queen loves flowers exceedingly, and she at once got ready and went with the King to the garden. At the time the Buddha was seated at the foot of a tree, and the Blessed One knowing that the Queen Khema was in the garden, created miraculously two beautiful young women standing on each side of the Blessed One fanning Him. Queen Khema at a distance saw the two beautiful figures, and

was astounded at their ravishing beauty, that she
forgot to think of her own self. Entranced by the
charming sight of the Buddha and the two women she
was unconsciously drawn towards them, and the
nearer she approached, she witnessed the two young
women gradually become old, and fell down dead,
and she realized that she was standing before the
Blessed One. She saw that beauty is only skin deep,
and she fell down at the feet of the Blessed One and
solicited ordination as a Bhikkhuni, and with the
consent of the King she joined the Holy Order, and
became the chief woman disciple in the Bhikkhuni
sāsana. She was appointed as the right hand woman
disciple of the Blessed One, an office as great as the
right hand discipleship which was held by the great
Sāriputra.

The famous simile of the chariot used by
Nāgasena to convince King Menander (Milinda) of the
non egoistic nature of the five skhandhas was used first
by the Bhikkhuni Vajirā in a discussion she had with
the King of Kosala. The famous sutta called the
"culla vedalla sutta," in the Majjhima nikāya. was
preached by the Bhikkhuni Dhammadinnā to her
husband, Who was less advanced than herself in the
comprehension of the psychological mysteries of the

159

cessation of sensations and perceptions, and her discourse received the approval of the Blessed One.

In ancient India there was a custom among the Brahmans to give the best education in philosophy to their daughters, and having finished their education they were allowed to visit any part of the Gangetic valley in search of husbands, and each one to marry the man who vanquishes her in open discussion. There were certain Brahmans who had mastered the science of physiognomy who went about examining men with the distinguishing marks of greatness to give their daughters in marriage to such. The Brahman Māgandhi and his wife were both professors of the science, and the Brahman one day saw the Buddha and from the great signs he thought he found the best man for his daughter, and approaching the Buddha told Him that he is willing to give his daughter to him, and asked him to wait, and he went home and told his wife that he has at last found a fit husband to their daughter; and the three came to the Buddha, who was at the time seated at the foot of a tree. The parents approached the Blessed One, and offered their daughter, and the Buddha preached the doctrine of decay, and refused to touch the daughter, whereupon the young woman was greatly offended. The man and wife became disciples of the Blessed One, but the daughter never forgave the Blessed One. Later on she was given to King Udeni as wife, and when Buddha visited the town she had the hooligans of the place bribed to abuse the Blessed One, when He was visiting the city.

When the princesses of Kapilavastu led by the foster mother and aunt of the Blessed One, Maha Prajāpati Gotami came to Him and requested permission to enter the homeless condition as Bhikkhunis, the Blessed One declined to admit them. He did not immediately accede to their wishes, the Commentator says, to discover how much strength of will power would they show to fulfil their cherished desire, and when the Blessed One left Kapilavastu for Vesali, the princesses headed by the Queen Prajapati came to Vesali walking all the way, so great was their desire to join the Order. The Blessed One thereupon acceded to their desire and the Bhikkhuni Order was established, of course within certain restrictions that they should always obey the Order of the Bhikkhu Sangha. It is the Bhikkhus who were to continue the work of proclaiming the Dhamma, and precedence was given to them inasmuch as the least of the Bhikkhu is worthy to be honoured by the most senior of the Bhikkhunis.

So long as the Religion of the Buddha was under

royal patronage and the Kings remained Buddhists, so
long the Bhikkhuni Order existed in India. We read
in the "Sri Harsha Charita." that the sister of King
Sri Harsha after the death of her husband joined the
Bhikkuni Order. The most learned of the Brahmans
at the time was the great Divākara, and he became a
Buddhist Bhikkhu.

The great lay woman Visākhā, the daughter of a
banker was chief among lay women in the religion of
the Buddha, She built the great Vihara to the east of
Jetavana at Sāvatthi.

The widow, and the fallen woman, the courtezan,
the young lady who did not want to marry, all found
a refuge in the Order of the Bhikkunis. The story of
the young mother Kisāgotami, who lost her first born
son shows how useful was the Bhikkhuni Order at the
time. The little boy was stung by a serpent and lay
dead, but she did not believe it and taking the dead
body was going from house to house asking people to
cure the boy. The people who saw the dead child,
said "go to the great physician, who is staying at
Jetavana, He will cure your child". and the weeping
mother taking the dead child, went to the Blessed One,
and showing the child said, "Great physician, I have
my sick child, cure him," and the Blessed One, said
"go, bring a handful of mustard seeds to cure the

162

child ;" and the weeping mother, glad at heart, started to go. and the Blessed One said "see that you get the mustard seed from a house, where no one had died", and she went from house to house, asking for mustard seed, and when the handful was given, she would ask, did any body die in this house ? and the answer was, "yes" ; and she would then return the handful of mustard seed. and go to another house, and she went from street to street, through the city, asking for mustard seed where no death had taken place, and at last she found that in the whole city of Sāvatthi there was not one house where there had not been a case of death. And her eyes were opened to the truth that nothing is permanent, and she threw away the dead body, and with a heart full of joy in having realized the truth, she came to the Blessed One, and said, Lord, I have found Truth, accept me as a disciple. This beautiful and touching story hath comforted millions of mothers in Buddhist lands since the occurrence of the event. Here in this story is the truth of the resurrection from death, not the regalvanizing of the dead body. A magician could galvanize a dead body and deceive the weeping mother. But he can give her no wisdom. The Blessed One gave ambrosia to the weeping mother, and she saw Truth, She received the Eye of

Truth (Dhamma cakkhu). Magicians give life to dead bodies, but they die again.

Two hundred years after the Parinibbāna of the Blessed One, the great and righteous Emperor Asoka, sent his daughter Sanghamittā in Ceylon to preach the Dharma and to found the Bhikkhuni Order. For nearly a thousand years it existed, and after that it ceased to exist. Woman as well as man can attain the perfection of Arhatship, in the power of grasping truth they are both equal. But in a woman's body no Buddha, no universal emperor, no Brahmā nor Indra appears.

Once a certain lay follower asked the great Arhat Sariputra whether his wife, who was then pregnant, would bring forth a male child, and Sariputra replied in the affirmative, but when the time came for her to deliver, she brought forth a female child ; and the discontented man went to the Blessed One and said that Sariputra was wrong in his prophesy. The Buddha said that Sariputra when he looked to foretell of the future child did dot look far enough. At the time that he was asked the embryo had not reached the stage of difierentiation. and Sariputra. without looking to the full period of development gave the answer. The Buddha thereupon laid down the law

164

that Bhikkhus should not go to foretell about child-births.

The duty of the woman is clearly laid down in the 8th Nipāta of the Auguttara Nikāya. She has her duties at home. She has to learn to be a help to her husband, she is expected to be clever in some kind of art or craft. The wife who is kind, and chaste and looks after the welfare of the husband after death is born in heaven. The cruel, unchaste, spendthrift of a wife after death is born in a place of suffering.

The clever, well behaved, learned woman, the Blessed One said may become the mother of a great King and also of a Buddha. Therefore no girl born should be despised said the Lord to the King of Kosala, who felt sorry when he heard that His wife the queen Mallikā gave birth to a daughter. The Buddha comforted the King. Educate the daughter in arts and morality, in religion, aud in domestic scinece (patibbatā, sīlavati, medhāvini) and she will give birth to good children. This is the law of Buddha.

Princess Yasodharā, the wife of the future Buddha, realized pari Nirvāna, a year before the parinibbāna of the Lord. For many million incarna-tions she was the wife of the Bodhisat life after life. Their love was not born in one life. The last life was the consummation of the deep desire that she had

cherished for one asankheyya kalpa. The horrid
doctrine that man should abandon his father and
mother and cling to his wife is abominably repulsive to
the Aryan mind. The Aryan husband trains his wife
to take care of his parents, and attend on holy men, on
his friends and relations. The glory of woman is in
her chastity, in the performance of household duties
and obedience to her husband. This is the Aryan
ideal wife. Husband and wife should be equal in
their understanding and wisdom, Both should be
chaste.

In the Maha Janaka Jātaka (Vol. IV.) the princess
receives a visit from a suitor, after the death of her
father whose last dying words to her that she should
marry a fit person, who will be able to manage the
kingdom ; and this personage was sent for and when
he came she told him kneel down, and he knelt
down, at her feet, and the princess thereupon thought
this fool is not fit to be my husband, and she ordered
her maids to have the man kicked out of her presence.
She wanted a person who had some kind of self
respect and not fall down at her feet. The Jātakas
contain about fifty stories about the characteristics of
woman, showing her good nature as well as her evil
nature. Aryan women have always held a supreme
place in the domestic economy of social progress. She

was ealled the "lady of the house" (gharasāmini) The ascetics did not like woman, but the poets sang of her beauty, and men of the world went mad after her.

In the history of religion there is only one faith that gave woman power to preach and to disseminate the faith, and that is the religion of the Blessed One. Other religions kept woman in the background. They were prohibited to speak before man.

THE WORK OF THE MAHA BODHI
SOCIETY

In the opinion of the late Professor Weber Buddhism was lost to India on account of its superior morality as it was too high for the degenerate people of the time. It does not take too long a period for a people to become irreligious. Take for instance modern Japan and compare her people forty years ago. The older generation knew not the demoralising materialism of industrial Japan. The modern Japanese, according to the view of scholars, have forgotten the ancient aesthetic morality for which Japanese of the old school were noted. Commercialism is taking the place of morality and religion. India began to lose her morality about nine hundred years ago. Amidst a luxurious civilization the Aryan people flourished, and their very prosperity made forget the high morality inculcated by the Aryan saviour.

Buddhism was forgotten, an impure ceremonialism crept in, and the people fell. Aryanism went down amidst the clash of arms and pagan sacrifices and the successive invasions of India by hordes of barbarians gave a death blow to the higher morality.

Modern Indians do not go beyond the period of

Sankara. To them ancient history is taboo. The stories of the Rāmāyana and Mahabharata are their history. The people of Bengal speak of the prophet of Nuddea, who re-established religion in the 15th century of the Christian Era. Beyond the period of Chaitanya the history of India is a blank. Moslem fanaticism and iconoclasm did much to destroy the historic foundations of India. India's ancient literature, her ancient aesthetic civilization, were totally obliterated by the hordes of invaders who came to plunder her immense wealth. After a thousand years India is on the threshold of a new era, but one thing she lacks, great spiritual leaders.

The Maha Bodhi Society is the first Buddhist organizations in the history of modern Buddhism to begin a propaganda for the dissemination of the Dharma in non-Buddhist lands. India had completely forgotten the Aryan doctrine of the Tathāgata, although at one time it held the foremost place among the Aryan religions in Aryavarta. For twenty-six years the Maha Bodhi Society has continued to exist in spite of the many obstacles, thanks to the generosity of a few friends of the Anagarika Dharmapala. The Society was founded by him in May, 1891, under the presidency of the late illustrious High Priest Sumangala of Ceylon, at Colombo.

In 1892 the Anagarika Dharmapala established the Journal of the Maha Bodhi Society, which is still in existence, and now being printed at Colombo in the Maha Bodhi Press. Owing to the paucity of Buddhists who are able to understand English in Buddhist countries the number of subscribers thereto is insufficient to make it pay. The Journal is sent free to the learned societies throughout the world as well as to the princes and nobles of Buddhist countries. For twenty years we are sorry to state the wealthy Buddhist dignitaries in Buddhist countries have failed to respond generously for the expansion of the objects of the Maha Bodhi Society. Japan and Siam have not helped by a single contribution for the furtherance of the noble objects of the society. Burma contributed generously at the commencement of operations of the society, but since sixteen years have failed to render any assistance. Several hundreds of subscribers to the Maha Bodhi Journal in Burma, India and Ceylon have failed to pay their subscriptions, and the loss thereby to the Journal amounts several thousand rupees.

The society had been able to erect two Dharma-sales at Buddhagaya and Saranath, Benares through the help of Buddhists of Burma, Arakan and Ceylon.

The Anagarika Dharmapala's mother, Srimati, Mallika Hevavitarana sent the first contribution of Rs. 600/- to purchase three acres of land at Sarnath, Benares.

The late Rajah of Bhinga contributed Rs. 2000/- which amount was expended in the purchase of ten bighas of land at Sarnath. The Society also has purchased a plot of land at Gaya, and it is lying idle as we have not the means of erecting a Dharmasala thereon for the use of pilgrims who visit Buddha Gaya. For nearly fifteen years efforts were made to get contributions to erect a Dharmasala from the well-to-do Buddhists, but we are sorry to say we have failed to find one Buddhist who is willing to contribute for the purpose.

Buddhists of Burma and Arakan, countries nearer to India, when written to for help, answers that they have no interest in India. China, Japan, Siam, independent Buddhist countries, when asked for help answer that charity begins at home. For nearly twenty years the society have received very little help from the people of Ceylon.

Buddhism the oldest and foremost of missionary religions has ceased to exist as a living force in the land of its birth, though its spirit still lingers. The last missionary went forth from Bengal in the person of

Srignāna Dipankara Atisa to reform the Buddhism of Tibet, nine hundred years ago. The Buddhism of Java was destroyed by the Arab Muhammedans about five hundred years ago. According to the researches of Archaeological scholars in Central Turkestan, Buddhism was a living religion in those distant lands a thousand years ago.

Archaeological evidence shows that Buddhist temples were built for the last time in Bengal and Magadha in the reign of Mahipala, king of Bengal in the eleventh century. In the beginning of the 13th century the university of Nalanda was destroyed by Bakhtyar Khilji.

The first vihar in Bengal that is going to be built will be erected in College Square, Calcutta, on the plot of land purchased at a cost of Rs. 22,000/-, which amount was contributed by the gracious lady, Mrs. T. R. Foster of Honolulu, Hawaii, in the Pacific ocean. The same lady has sent a further contribution of Rs. 35,000/- to build the vihar. The Anagarika Dharmapala met the lady at Honolulu on the 18th of October, 1893 ; from his mouth she heard the doctrine of the Blessed One, and she was comforted, and in a spirit of thankfulness she is helping the Angarika to revive Buddhism in India since 1904.

In the ancient days when Buddhism was the

religion of the land, and the king became one with people, it was a common thing to see the king building a temple in memory of the Buddha. The great Emperor Asoka, it is said, erected 84000 temples throughout his empire, and some of the temples that he ordered to be erected are still visible in different parts of India. Under the Muhammedan rule it was not possible for the Buddhist of other lands to enter India, and the building of new temples to Buddha was not attempted. After a long period extending over seven hundred years the opportunity has come for the Buddhists to enter India and revive the long forgotten religion under the gracious protection of the British Government. To build the first temple in Calcutta it was found necessary to appeal to both Buddhists and Hindus, and a printed circular accompanied by a letter received from the Government of India about the building of the vihara in Calcutta to enshrine the Buddha relic was sent to the King of Siam, the only Buddhist king. Sevaral appeals were made to His Majesty pointing out the peculiar position of the Buddhists in India. No answer was received direct from the Siamese government, and we are informed that no help will be given by the Siamese for the construction of the first Vihara in Calcutta. When

India was Buddhistic, her kings and the Bhikkhus of the Lord Buddha helped the Mongolian races to receive the gift of the Dharma and the culture of India was freely given. Now that India is in need, the response that the Indian Buddhists get from distant Buddhist countries is not of a cheering nature. The King of Siam is a Buddhist, and is styled "Defender of the Faith ;" we do sincerely trust that help will be forthcoming from him and the Rajahs and Maharajahs in India to build a worthy Vihara to enshrine the Relic of the Buddha which the Government of India has been graciously pleased to present to the Maha Bodhi Society.

WAR LOAN.

The Anagarika Dharmapala as Trustee of the Mrs. T. R. Foster Fund has invested Rs. 18,000/- in War Bonds, and requested the Dewan of His Highness the Maharajah of Baroda to buy War Bonds for the sum of Rs. 5,000/- and the Dewan has written to say that the Maha Rajah Saheb has agreed to do so. The Anagarika has also further invested Rs. 9,000/- in War Bonds of the Vihara Fund. Last year on behalf of the Maha Bodhi Society he contributed Rs. 1,000/- to the Carmichael War Fund.

174

THE WORK OF MAHA BODHI SOCIETY.

THE PLAN OF THE VIHARA

Sir John Marshall, Director General of Archaeo-logy, has kindly prepared ths plan of the proposed Vihara. The design is based on the Ajanta temple architecture, and is exquisitely done. When the temple is erected it will be an object of attraction in Calcutta. We have to thank Sir John Marshall for the kind services graciously rendered. It will require at least a lakh of rupees to complete the building according to the design. We therefore hope that those who love the Lord Buddha will, a cheerful heart, freely give to the Vihara Fund.

It is a matter of astonishment that whilst a lady from the extremely distant land of Hawaii is joyously contributing to built the Vihara to the memory of the Saviour of Humanity of the Aryan race, Buddhists of Japan, China, Siam, Burma, Ceylon have failed to respond to the appeal issued by the Maha Bodhi Society. The invariable answer is that they have no interest in India. The gracious lady Mrs. T. R. Foster has already contributed Rs. 35,000/- and the Anagarika Dharmapala Rs. 10,000/-.

The Government of India has consented to present the Bhattiprolu relic of the Buddha also to the Maha Bodhi Society to be enshrined at Saranath,

Benares, and the Government expect that a worthy vihara shall be built there. Mrs. T. R. Foster has graciously contributed for the construction of the Saranath Vihara the sum of Rs. 18,000/-. This sum was contributed several years ago, before the Government of India had decided to present the Buddha relic to the Society.

At Saranath, the holy place where 2505 years ago the Lord Buddha preached the first sermon of the Nirvana Doctrine, there is a Museum of Buddhist Sculptures built at a cost of about Rs. 60,000/- by the Government of India. It is hoped that within a few years the Maha Bodhi Society will be able to make the place a centre of Buddhist literary studies. When the Hindu University is built, let us hope that Buddhism and Hinduism will join hands at Benares and work for the salvation of the World.

"Not by hatred does hatred cease ; by love Hatred ceases" taught the Lord Buddha. He taught us that we should

"Conquer hatred by love
Conquer evil by righteousness
Conquer the liar by truthfulness
Conquer the greedy by charity."

Not by destruction but by love can reforms be

176

brought about. The time wasted in destruction may well be spent in the altruistic work of self-sacrifice. The Bhikkhus of old-wearing the yellow robe gave their learning free, and they taught the village people and their children the arts and sciencs, and each village was at a centre of literary activity. The village temple, the village dharmasala, the village school, the village playground, the village tank, the village park, the village tribunal came into existence where the Buddha's Bhikkhus settled. Self control is the basic doctrine of the Buddha. "Atta dipā viharatha atta saranā anañña saranā."

The Buddha wisdom is to be found in the three Pitakas, and they contain the ancient Aryan ethics, philosophy, psychology, history, of India. This store-house of learning was the inheritance of the people of ancient India, but to-day this precious heirloom is not to be found in India. For 2000 years Ceylon had been preserving the sacred treasure, and the time is now come that this gem should be again brought back to India. Pāli has become a subject of study in the Calcutta University, and the Maha Bodhi Society was the first to start a Pāli class, and to publish the first Pāli Grammar, sixteen years ago. The name of Satis Chandra Vidyabhusana shall ever be associated with the efforts of the Maha Bodhi Society as the pioneer of Pāli learning in India. When the millions of young Indians learn Pāli then will come the glorious dawn of an Indian renaissance. The gods exist, but the Buddha gives wisdom to erring mortals.

The Maha Bodhi Society sincerely hope that the wealthy sons of mother India will make an effort to print in Devanagri the Pitaka texts. The Jataka stories are of perennial interest to the students of ancient Indian history. When they are translated into Hindi and Bengalee, and other Indian vernaculars the village folk will find in them a garden of aesthetic delight, For the sake of the teeming millions of India's ignorant people, we hope that a systematic effort will be made to translate the Jatakas. The British people, the noblest of all modern races, have the 500 Jataka stories in English garb. The indefatigable scholars Professor and Mrs. Rhys Davids have published the larger part of the Pāli texts in Roman character. A large number of sutras have been translated into English by them. Bhikkhu-Silāchara, a Scotchman converted to Buddhism, is working vigorously in Rangoon in translating the Buddha sutras into English. Throughout Europe scholars are engaged in either editing or translating the sutras of the Lord Buddha. Sir Charu Chandra Bose has translated the "Dhammapada" into Bengali.

The Bengal Buddhist Association is working vigorously for the welfare of Chittagong Buddhists, under the leadership of Kiripa Thero and Swami Punnānanda.

It is a melancholy fact that only the Buddhists are inactive in spreading the teachings of the Master in foreign lands. There are nearly a millon of Bhikkhus in all Buddhist lands, but these are of no help to the world. He who does not work hard to increase the sum of human happiness, lives his life in vain. Greater than the bliss of sweet Nirvana is the life of moral activity. The Blessed One worked daily for 22 hours, from His 35th year to His 80th year. For siz years He made the supreme struggle in the forest to gain knowledge. The ancient Rishis counted time in years, but our Lord counted time by hours. An hour under the Dispensation of the Buddha is equal to a year and the Gospel of Activity was what He preached day after day for 16200 days, and each day He was engaged in doing good to the world of gods and men for twenty-two hours. During the forty-five years His blessed life was spent for 256400 hours in workiug for the welfare of the world, and the results of His labours are still visible, and shall remain visible for centuries to come, provided there were youngmen of self-sacrificing devotion to follow the glorious example.

179

Since July, 1891, the Anagarika has made every effort to bring back the forgotten Doctrine of the Tathagata. Single handed, without the support of monarchs and wealthy Buddhists, for 26 years He has toiled on patiently, full of hope that when the time arrives India's best sons will take up the banner of the Buddha's Love and preach His Gospel of Wisdom and Love to the millions of India, What the teeming millions need is Enlightenment. Love, compassion, unselfishness are the essential qualities needed in the Indian teacher to ameliorate the conditions of the teeming millions.

If all Indians would contribute a couple of lakhs of rupees to the Maha Bodhi Society, the full programme for the revival of this religion of Compassion and Wisdom in the land of Buddha's birthcould be put into effect. India has an abundance of gods, what she reqnires is wisdom. The opponents of the Buddha say that he did not preach the existence of God. but the Brahmans say that He is God incarnate. How could then God preach to another God ? The other avatars of Vishnu, like Rama and Krishna are not accused of being atheists. How could the Buddha be charged as an athiest, and yet be acknowledged as God incarnate.

The Buddha came to fulfil, to purify, to increase

180

the sum of human happiness, and He taught the Way
thereto, which He called The Middle Path. Speculations of the Whence, Why and the Whither have no
place in His scientific Doctrine based on the immutable law of cause and effect and the law of Karma.
He rejected all beliefs that posited a permanent
separate soul. and condemned systems that taught
nihilistic views. He who has no fear of the future
world and who is given to the enjoyment of sense
pleasures. our Lord declared, may not receive His
teachings, but those who are given to serious thought
and are earnest in the search after truth, they shall
certainly hear it. The teachings of the Tathagata are
simple and were expressed in one gathā.

Avoid all evil (in thought word and deed)
Ceaselessly do good (in thought deed and words)
Make the heart radiant (by means of samādhi)
Such are the teachings of Buddhas.

———

THE DEVELOPMENT OF ARTS, INDUSTRIES AND AGRICULTURE

The Lord Buddha made indolence a sin producing evil karma. Activity in arts. literature, service, agriculture was commended as righteous and productive of good karma. Karma is action. either good or bad. Results productive of good were called the fruits of good karma (karmaphala). To sweep the place and keep it clean was a good act and producing good karma. To allow dirt to accumulate and not have it removed after having seen it, is productive of bad karma. To please the aesthetic feelings of others is good, and is productive of good karma. To build a rest house for the public good, to build a bridge, to put up lights in a place for the benefit of others, to help the poor, to take care of parents, and holy men. yellow robed Ascetics and Brahmans, to show hospitality to strangers, to nurse the sick, to be courteous to elders, to take care of orphans, to establish free hospitals, and rest-houses to preach the good law, to hear the good law, to keep the mind upright in accordance with the law of righteousness. to show kindness to all living beings, to prevent cruelty to animals, to take care of the aged animals, to disseminate the good law,—all these are productive of good karma,

To be indifferent to the sufferings of others, to live untidily, and to allow dirt and filth to accumulate and not have them removed, to be indolent and postpone work that requires immediate attention are productive of evil karma. It is called gehasita upekkhā, domestic indifference leading to misery.

A kind thought, a good word spoken. a deed of charity however small produce good karma. Man is like a karma producing dynamo. Indifference leads to stagnation of mind, and evil deeds lead to degeneration and arrest the development of consciousness leading towards animality. Man has behind him a storage of karma which is called aparāpariya vedaniya karma, which is a kind of potential karma waiting to come into operation whenever the opportunity occurs.

Many are the similes used by the Blessed One to expound His teachings . Kammam khettam, viññāṇam bijam. Here the word khettam connotes field, and bija is seed. Karma is like unto a field, and viññāna (consciousness) is like the seed ; architectural phrases are also used to illustrate the teachings.

THE ARYA DHARMA OF GAUTAMA, THE BUDDHA.

Activity in the field of arts, industries and agriculture lead to the accumulation of good karma, and
they are classified under the category of right livelihood (sammā ājivo). One Bhikkhu while superin-
tending the building of a vihāra became an arhat. He
was before he joined the Holy Order an architect.
Cullapantha became an arhat by contemplating on
the lotus flower, and in his last birth he was a gold-
smith, and the Blessed One saw by His divine eye
as to the kind of upanissaya karmma of Cullapantha,
and he found it out, and gave him the lesson to
contemplate on aesthetic art represented in the lotus
flower.

Four requisites which the Blessed One ordained
for a Bhikkhu are robes, food, seats and residences,
and medicaments. Everything in domestic and social
economics are included in the four categories,
Garments to wear, how to produce them ? Cotton is
required, and to obtain yarn cotton has to be cultivated. Millions of robes were requird yearly for the
Bhikkhus when Buddhism was a living religion in
India. The Bhikkhu required an antaravāsa, uttarā-
sangha, a sanghāti, a nisidana, a vassa-sāṭaka and
nāna-sataka. Hand loom weaving was an industry
greatly fostered during the Buddhist period. To make
a kaṭina civara, the cotton had to be twisted into yarn,

and the cloth woven on the same day, and dyed and sewn. To feed the thousands and thousands of Bhikkhus rice was necessary, and large tracts of land were set apart by the kings to be brought under cultivation to plant paddy, and along with agriculture cattle keeping was greatly encouraged, and dairying was a great industry in the Buddhist period, for milk, butter and butter oil were largely used by the Bhikkhus as food. The construction of viharas, bhojanasālas, gilana-sālas, vaccakuti, passāvakutī, mandaps, cloisters, divāsthānas. rātristhānas, udaka-sālas, parivenas, uposatha halls, upasthāna-halls, tanks, helped to advance the science of architecture and the walls were painted with scenes and this helped the development of painting. The Blessed One did not believe in driving out devils when His Bhikkhus fell sick. He inculcated the use of medicine, and the science of medicine was cultivated by the Bhikkhus for their own use. Every Vihāra had a gilāna sālā where the sick Bhikkhus were treated. The Buddha Himself attended on the sick Bhikkhus. Medical science it the Buddhist period was very progressive. The Bhikkhus had to study the dead body in their meditations in various phases of decomposition. Where-ever the Bhikkhus went they carried culture along with them.

THE ARYA DHARMA OF GAUTAMA, THE BUDDHA.

When the great mission headed by the Princess missionary Sanghamittrā was sent by the great Emperor Asoka to Ceylon, the good emperor sent experts in all kinds of arts and industries, as part of the mission. Eighteen kinds of arts and industries were represented in the mission to Ceylon. Sculpture, horticulture. floriculture, weaving, &c., were introduced into Ceylon by the good emperor 2220 years ago. But for Buddhism to-day there would be nothing ancient and aesthetic in the world, except the mummies and Egyptian and Babylonian archaelogical remnants. Where Buddhism went there was diffused culture. Painting, architecture, agriculture. textile industries, temperance flourished in Buddhist countries. Other religions destroy culture and spread intemperance. Destruction is the law of other religions. The scriptures of Monotheistic religions inculcate destruction and desuetude. The Vedas are only for the high caste, and the Sudra is to be robbed of whatever good things he has, according to the Brahmanical laws of Manu, Apastamba Yajnāvalkya, Nārada and Gautama. Two thousand years ago the great Emperor Asoka caused the viharas to be built in various parts of India, and to-day the archaeological scholar admires and writes monographs. In Ceylon,

186

Burma, China, Tibet, and Japan art flourished extensively under Buddhism. The following quotation from a work brought out by the erudite scholar Dr. M. Anesaki of Japan will show to what extent Art and Buddhism go together :

"Curiously there prevails in the West an impression that Buddhism is a religion of mere negation and pure abstraction. Here I shall not argue. I simply wish to point out that he will never understand Buddhist art who does not free his mind from such a preconception. Buddhism exhorts its followers to overstep the bounds of self and enter the ideal community of spiritual life. This teaching is, to be sure, a negation of the bondage of individual limitations ; but it is equally an affirmation of a life broader than the individual. It may be called withdrawal from the material world, but it is also an entrance into the larger world of ideals. It was this breadth of mental vista and depth of sympathy that made Buddhism a universal religion and gave inspiration to artistic genius. The ideal of the Buddhist faith consists in realizing, through spiritual experience and in moral acts, the continuity of life in man and nature and the fellowship of all beings. This ideal was the soil which nourished the stem of the Buddhist religion and the flowers of

187

Buddhist art......The Buddha became the fountain head of an inexhaustible inspiration in religion and morals, in art and poetry......perceived in man and nature the vital and sympathetic tie which bound them to his own soul. Nothing is left outside the bounds of his sympathy ; all is viv.fied by the touch of personal relation. This is the process of idealization, the secret of artistic creation ; and Buddha grasped this secret in his conception of universal communion and through his training in the transformed life...... Buddhism is by no means a religion of mere ecstacy. Its meditative training, together with the practice of charity in various ways, results in a total transformation of life through the realization first in ideas and then in acts, of one's spiritual connexion and sympathetic accord with mankind and surrounding nature. "The realization of a universal spiritual communion is the fundamental ideal of the Buddhist religion. It was this ideal that gave Buddhism the power of expansion beyond the boundaries of nations fired its adherents with missionary zeal, and inspired the imagination of its artists and poets. One who can appreciate this ideal will understand Buddhist art, and will discover in the hearts of the Japanese a tone of tenderness and a depth of sympathy which are the essential conditions of artistic creation and enjoyment.

(p. 30). Buddhist temples were places not only of worship but also of learning, where philosophy and music were taught and moral discipline was inculcated. Moreover charitable institutions. such as hospitals, infirmaries and dispensaries, were attached to them, as means of putting the Buddhist ideal of universal love into actual practice. The whole foundation thus served as a focus of the Buddhist religion, morality and art which now became integral parts of the national life, (p. 21) The Buddhist gospel of an all-embracing spiritual communion which could be realized in human life, was preached to the East and West, imbuing its converts everywhere with an aspiration for universal communion"......(p. 19).— "Buddhist Art in Its Relation to Buddhist Ideas." London : John Murray.

BUDDHA-GAYA, THE HOLIEST
BUDDHIST SHRINE

What Benares is to the Saivites, what Vishnupad
at Gaya is to both Saivites and Vaisnāvites, what
Mecca is to the Muhammedans, what Jerusalem is to
the Christians and Jews, that Buddha-gaya is to the
Buddhists of the World. The Blessed One sanctified
the holy spot by the gratitude He had shown to the
Tree, under whose shade He sat on the full moon day
of the month of Baisakh, 2506 years ago, when He
became the

"Saviour of the world
Lord Buddha, Prince Siddhartha styled on Earth,
In Earth, and Heavens and Hells Incomparable
All-honoured, Wisest, Best, most Pitiful
The Teacher of Nirvāna and the Law."

Light of Asia.

The Blessed One said that Bhikkhus, Bhikkhunis,
Upāsakas and Upāsikās who visit the four sanctified
places of the birth, Buddhahood, preaching the Law
and His final Parinirvāna, viz., Kapilavastu, Bodhimanda, Benares and Kusinārā, and who meet with
their death are born in heaven. See Mahāparinibbāna
sutta and Anguttara nikāya.

190

The holy spot so sacred to the Buddhists after receiving the homage of the millions of Buddhists of the whole Buddhist world for eighty generations, went into decay after the place was destroyed by the invader of Bengal, the Mohammedan general Bakhtiyar Khilji in the year 1202 A.C.

The great Asoka commemorated his visit to the sacred shrine by a memorial sculpture which is to be found to-day in the torana at Sanchi. The great Emperor visiting the place in procession and alighting from the back of the elephant within the precincts of the Bodhi Tree is beautifully depicted. The royal banner with the Buddhist symbol, the royal standard, and musicians are all sculptured with care, and after two thousand years we are able to understand what a Buddhist procession was like 2200 years ago under imperial patronage.

Vincent Smith in his "Early History of India" says "the furious massacres perpetrated in many places by Musulman invaders were more efficacious than orthodox Hindu persecutions, and had a great deal to do with the disappearance of Buddhism in several provinces". pp. 354, 968, 404.

The so-called persecutions conducted by Sankara in the seventh century A.C. have no historic foundations. Under the great Pāla dynasty which ended in the tenth century, Buddhism was the state religion throughout Northern India and Bengal. The history of Kasmir shows that in the tenth century there were Buddhist temples in that land. The inscriptions discovered at Sravasti shows that in the beginning of the 12th century of the Christian era the holy spot at Jetavana was under the custody of Buddhist monks. The inscriptions at Sarnath and Buddha-gaya show that there had been great and extensive repairs and fresh decorations in the holy spots under the guidance of King Mahipala. A religion that lived side by side with the religion of Siva and Vishnu for nearly a thousand years, in whose temples the images of the gods worshipped by the followers of Siva and Vishnu were incorporated for many generations, a religion under the greatest of Indian kings was made a state religion, whose patrons were the Kshatriya princes claiming relationship with the Buddha who was descended from the royal line of Ikhsvaku of the solar dynasty, that after it had become a part of the life of the Indian people, should be destroyed at the word of a Kerala Dravidian Brahman, who was driven out of his own province because he was considered the son of a mother who had no husband, is impossible to believe. A religion that moulded the destinies of the nation for so many centuries, that gave a culture, an incomparable code of moral laws, that made the people a harmonious whole, should be destroyed simply to satisfy a sectarian, Brahman, no historian would accept. There is nothing in Buddhism that was repulsive to the Brahmans. The best of the Brahmans were the foremost of the Buddha's disciples. The Buddha had emphasised in His great Utterances in the Itivuttaka the great help the Brahmans gave to the Bhikkhus of His Religion in providing them with food, robes, residences, &c. The writers of polemics never had known the similarities that existed between the religion of the Barhmans and the Buddha, and failing to find evidences to show the causes of the final disappearance of the great religion found it wes easy to give the credit to Sankara.

Curiously in the Padmapurāna there is a passage which the puranic writer puts into the month of Siva that he incarnated to teach the doctrine know as the Vedānta, which is no other than the doctrine of the Bauddhas who are naked and who wear blue graments.

"Bauddhasastram asat proktam nagna nilapata' dikam
Mayavadam asac chastram pracchannam bauddham eva ca"

Now in Buddhist scriptures nakedness is storngly condemned, and no Bhikkhu is allowed by the vinaya

M   193

rules to speak to a naked ascetic. No Buddhist
Bhikkhu is allowed to wear a blue garment. The
passage refers to a sect of the Jainas who are known
as digambaras and to a heretical sect who wore blue
garments "Nila pata vastra."

Buddhism was destroyed by the invaders from
Arabia· They had before coming over to India seen
the beautiful temples in Gandhāra, Turfun, Turkestan,
which they had destroyed, and they had known by
sight the thousands of the images of the Buddha which
they had smashed to pieces in their vandalic career,
and they had heard the name of Buth—the Buddha—;
and when they entered the holy land of the Buddhists
they found wherever they went images of the Buddha
in temples. The hated Buth image was demolished,
and along with the Buddha images idols of Vishnu,
Siva, Ganesh, and other gods of the Puranic
pantheon were mutilated.

The Bodhi Tree was the central shrine of all
Buddhist nations. The king of Ceylon Sri Megha-
varma in the fourth century of the Christian Era casued
to be built a great Sangharāma which was admired by
all who visited the holy spot. Hwen Thsang in the
seventh century saw it and he describes it in his
Tarvels.

In the Tibetan work called "Vinaya pushpa

194

mālā" it is mentioned that when the Turuskas invaded Magadha, the Buddhist monks carried away the holy image of the Buddha from the Buddha-gaya temple and had it hidden in the forest. In 1202 the vandals began to destroy the temples and universities in Magadha and Mithila The Nālandā university which had a student population of near ten thousand and the temples which had thousands of yellow robed Bhikkhus were all destroyed, and the monks massacred. The university of Mithila is mentioned in the Tibetan history as a place where the Tibetan monks came to learn Buddhism. In Taxila, Benares, Kanouj, Sravasti, Ujjeni, Sanchi, Ajantā, Kusināra, Mathura and in Kasmir there were thousands of Bhikkhus. Literature, art works, and the accumulated wealth of nearly two thousand years were destroyed and removed respectively. The Hun invader Mihiri-kula destroyed Taxila, but did not come over to India proper.

The Buddha was worshipped by the Vaishnavas as the ninth avatar of the God Vishnu. The following works of the Purānic literature are quoted to show how much the Buddha was part of the Brahmanical worship :—Vāyu Purāna Uttarardha, Lessen 43, v. 26-29; Agni Purāna, Lesson 115, v. 37 ; Bhāgavata, Skandha. 6, Lesson 8, v. 17 ; Agni Purāna, Lesson 49, v. 2-8 ;

Nirnaya sindhu, Lesson II.; Bhavishya Purāna Uttarārdha, Lesson 73; Hemādri, Lesson 15, Vrata khanda; Barahā Purāna, Lesson 48, v. 22; Matsya Purāna, Ch. 47, v. 247; Garuda Purāna, Section 202, v. 11; Devi bhāgavata, skanda 10, Ch. 5, v. 14; Padma Purāna, kriya khanda Ch. 6, v. 188; Nārada-pancha rātra, sāktapramāda; Sankara-vijaya, Sec. 12 v. 8; Dasāvatāra khanda prasasti; Gitagovinda.

Buddha-gaya for centuries after the place was destroyed by the Moslem invaders remained neglected when in the eighteenth century the place went under the custody of the Saivite mahants. In 1833 March, a Burmese embassy came to Buddha-gaya to restore the shrine. Then in the time of the late King Mindoon of Burma an Agent of the King came to Buddha-gaya and began to repair the temple. In 1877 the Government of India with the consent of the King of Burma began the work of complete restoration and finished the work in 1880. In 1880 the late King Thibaw sent Burmese monks to remain in the Burmese rest house which was erected under orders of the King.

In October, 1885, when the King was deposed by the British the Burmese monks and the Agent left Buddha-gaya for Burma.

From 1885 to 1890 the Temple and the Resthouse

were neglected, and in April 1890 the Collector of Gaya, Mr. Grierson, now Sir George, wrote to the Government about the temple and had a custodian appointed to take charge of the temple and the rest-house.

In January, 1891, the Anagarika Dharmapala came to Buddha-gaya on a pilgrimage and seeing the place neglected adopted measures to restore the holy site and to have Buddhist monks stationed permanently. He wished to continue the work of the late king of Burmah. He remained at the holy spot and began correspondence with the Buddhists of Ceylon. Burma, Siam, Japan, china, Arakan, Chittagong and in May, 1891, the Maha Bodhi Society was established under the presidentship of the late illustrious High Priest Sumangala.

In July, 1891, Bhikkhus were brought from Ceylon and were placed in the Burmese resthouse with the consent of the Collector and with his sympathy.

In 1892, May, the Maha Bodhi Journal was started by the Anagarika which is now in its 25th year. in 1892, October, the Calcutta head quarters of the society were established with the help of the Buddhists of Akyab. They contributed to the Buddha-gaya fund Rs. 5,000 out of which the sum of Rs. 2500 was paid to the Indian work, and the balance is still in the hands of the Arakan Buddhists, Efforts were made to recover this amount from the trustees for the work in India but without result. In 1893, June, the Anagarika started to attend the Chicago Parliament of Religions which was held in September, 1893. In August, 1893, the Anagarika went to London to meet the late Sir Edwin Arnold on behalf of the Buddhists of Ceylon, and they both went to see the Secretary of State for India, Earl Kimberley, who promised to look into the matter of the Buddha-gaya restoration.

In June, 1892, a meeting of Buddhists took place at Darjiling and the Anagarika Dharmapala delivered a message to the Bnddhists of Tibet and presented a Relic of the Buddha in an ancient ivory dagoba to be sent to the Dalai Lama of Lhasa. The relic was not sent.

In September, 17, 1893, the Anagarika as the Delegate of the Ceylon Buddhists made his address at the Congress of Religions, In October, 18, 1893, at Honolulu on board the Occanic, Mrs. T. R. Foster and her friends met the Anagarika, and in November he landed at Tokyo and was the guest of the Buddhists. The High priest Asahi of the Tentokuji temple with the concurrence of the Buddhists of his church presented the famous image of the Buddha to be enshrined at the Buddha-gaya temple, having heard that there was on image on the altar of the upper storey thereof. It was the article that appeared in the Maha Bodhi Journal of September, 1893, that prompted the high priest to present the Image. The article was a translation of the chapter from the Vinaya pushpa mālā, quoted above. The Image was sent to Ceylon thence to Calcutta and it was taken to Buddha-gaya in April, 1894.

In January, 1894, the Anagarika Dharmapala along with the Revd. Timothy Richard and Dr. Franke visited the Buddhist Temple near Shanghai and presented a relic of the Buddha to the priests and asked their co-operation for the restoration of the Buddha Gaya temple.

In February, 1894, the Anagarika Dharmapala visited Bangkok, Siam, and was received very kindly by the princes, and the late king Chulalongkorn at the time was very ill. The Anagarika delivered a message before the princes and people at the royal library and the Prime Minister Prince Devavongsa Varoprakar sent an autograph letter promising a contribution of Rs. 150 per month for the expenses of the society. This sum was never contributed, and the visit to Siam ended in failure. The answer invariably came that charity begins at home, and for twenty-five years nothing was received from the Government of

Siam. The late Prince Sommot Amarabandhu was a friend of the Society and occasionally small donations came from the good prince. The Journal was sent free to many of the English speaking princes for 24 years. In 1896 there was a movement started to raise a lakh of rupees to buy the Mahabodhi land, but owing to want of sympathy with the Buddha-gaya work the movement failed. The ethic of charity has yet to be learnt by the Budhhists of Siam. Charity begins at home it is true, but it must not end there. The Buddhas show compassion to the ignorant. The ancestors of the present Buddhists of Siam were converted to Buddhism by Aryan Buddhists who had compassion on the people. If the Buddhists won't help the work surely we could not expect non-Buddhists to help the propagation of the Dharma. If Buddhists have faith in the Buddha, they will think of the Lord and they will then know the great Spirit of compassion which prompted Him to renounce a kingdom to work for the salvation of the world. If the Buddhists know the Dhamma they would then make supreme efforts to make others Buddhists. They are ignorant of the sublime beauties of the noble Aryan religion, and when attacked by foreign missionaries they have no answer to give. They are foolishly silent. Buddhists of Asia should abandon the path of selfishness and follow the path of compassion and show activity. Where there is no activity there is death. Pamādo maccuno padam.

In April, 1894, the Japanese Image was to have been enshrined at the temple at Buddha-gaya, but the Mahant was obstinate in his refusal and the Image could not be enshrined.

In September, 1894, the Anagarika Dharmapala went to Ceylon and raised Rs. 35,000 from the Buddhists of Ceylon to purchase the Maha Bodhi village at Buddha-gaya. A lakh of rupees was required but the amount could not be raised. The Burmese Buddhists raised Rs. 13,000.

In February, 1895, the Japanese Image was taken to the temple and placed on the shrine, but the menials of the saivite mahant came and had the Image removed and put it in the open. The Collector advised the Anagariks to institute legal proceedings against the saivite priests, and the case known as the Buddha-gaya temple case was heard in the courts at Gaya, and the High Court Judges declared that the Image was placed in a place where worship was not carried on, although according to the laws of Buddhist worship every part of the shrine is sacred. The Buddhists lost the case, and the Image was removed

to the Burmese resthouse. The Saivite mahant thereupon moved that the Burmese resthouse was his
property and that the Japanese Image should not be
kept there, and the Commissioner of Patna directed
the Collector of Gaya to have the Image removed from
the resthouse. Mr. Savage the Collector sent an
ultimatum to the General Secretary of the M. B. S.
to have the Image removed at once, and unless
it is removed within 24 days the Government of
Bengal will have it removed to the Indian Museum
and kept there as a derelict. The Geneaal Secretary
thereupon communicated with the Burmese Buddhists
in Rangoon to represent to the Government of Burma
that the Resthouse was built by the King of Burma,
and that the Buddhists have a right to place the
Image. The representations made were convincing
and the Bengal Government passed orders that the
Japanese Image should be allowed to remain in
the Resthouse. The Lieutenant-Governor of Bengal
at the time was Sir Alexander Macenzie. The
Buddhists of Ceylon spent for the Bud-gaya case
Rs. 25,000 from the Buddha-gaya Fund.

In 1896, the Anagarika left India on a long tour for
the United States and travelled many thousand miles
in giving lectures on Buddhism, and in 1897 he visited
Europe and attended the Congress of Orientalists at

Paris and delivered a speech there, and also held a Buddhist festival at the Musee Guimet, which was attended by a number of very aristocratic Parisians. He travelled in Italy and returned to Ceylon in October 1897. In this absence the British Indian Association urged the Bengal Government to have the Japanese Image removed from the Burmese Rest-house. The Government replied that the request cannot be granted. In 1898 the Anagarika made a long tour in Northern India giving lectures in various towns, and he visited the Buddhist ruins in the Cabul valley, In 1902 he visited Japan and the United States and spent one year in the latter country in giving lectures on Buddhism. He wrote to **Mrs.** Foster to open an industrial school at Benares, and the good lady made a grant of Rs. 8,000.

In 1901 the General Secretary represented matters to the Collector of Gaya, Mr. C. E. A. Oldham, that the pilgrims visiting Bud-gaya were put to indes-cribable inconveniences in not having a kitchen and bath and privies, and that in Buddhist countries dogs receive better and more kind treatment than the pilgrims at Bud-gaya. This had effect on the good Collector and he moved that the Gaya District and should acquire land from the saivite mahant and build a resthouse at Buddha-gaya in common for both

Buddhists and Hindus. This information was con-
veyed to the General Secretary by the Hony. Legal
Adviser of the M. B. S, Babu Nanda Kishore Lall,
who suggested that the Society should provide funds
to build a resthouse exclusively for the Buddhists. The
General Secretary thereupon wrote to the Collector
who accepted the offer. In October, 1901, the good
Lieut.-Governor of Bengal visited Buddha-gaya and
received an address from the Maha Bodhi Society
under the shade of the sacred Bodhi Tree, and he
promised to grant the request of the Buddhists.
Where is the money to come from to build the
Dharmasāla ? The Burmese Buddhists had raised in
1893 Rs. 13,000, and this money was still lying in the
Bank at Mandalay, and the General Secretary went to
Mandalay and got the money from the President of
the Mandalay Maha Bodhi Society and remitted to the
Government of Bengal. For full ten years the General
Secretary struggled hard to get this done, and
perseverance and energy triumphed and the Rest-
house was completed in 1903. The thanks of the
Buddhists of all countries are due to the Collector Mr.
Oldham, to the good Governor Sir John Woodburn,
and to Babu Nanda Kishore Lall and to the Mandalay
Maha Bodhi Society. The plan was designed by the
Anagarika Dharmapala and the sum of Rs. 15,000

was spent on the building ; Rs. 2000 being contributed by the Ceylon Maha Bodhi Society.

Anagarika visited several countries and lectured in various places and returned to India in April 1904. In November, 1904, he returned to Ceylon hearing that his father was dangerously ill, and in his absence enemies of Buddha-gaya worked to ruin the interests of the Buddhists at the holy shrine. Japanese by the name of Okakura, visited India in 1903 and associated with a number of Bengalees to establish a centre of Japanese Buddhism at Buddha-gaya. He with the help of the Bengalees, of the party belonging to a neo-Hindu school opened negotiations with the saivite mahant stating that Japanese Buddhism is similar to Hinduism, and that they have no relationship with the Buddhists of Ceylon, and urged the mahant to grant the Japanese a plot of land at Buddha-gaya to build a Japanese temple. At the same time other agencies were at work against the Maha Bodhi Society. In 1905 another Society under the name of the Buddhist Shrines Restoration Society was formed at calcutta with a view to supercede the Maha Bodhi Society, and as it received the support of the Bengal Government many influential Buddhists joined it. The Society forgot the work of the M. B. S. which it had accomplished since 1891, and negotiated with the Mahant arranging certain conditions which were inimical to Buddhist interests, The General Secretary was in Ceylon and the Buddhist Restoration Society was working with apparent vigour. Captain O'Conor was the Secretary, and the late Maharaja of Sikkhim was the president. The M. B. S. lost the sympathy of the Burmese friends on account of the malicious representations of certain persons in Rangoon. Things were all dark, In 1906 the Commissioner of Patna work to the General Secretary who was them in Ceylon, expressing sentiments of condemnation of Buddhist activity at Buddha-gaya, and in June 1906 Mr. Levinge, Commissioner of Patna visited and advised the saivite Mahant to institute a civil suit against the Buddhists and have them ejected from the Burmese Resthouse. The Mahant having received encouragement from Government brought a civil suit against the Maha Bodhi Society and summons were issued in September 1906 against the Anagarika Dharmapala and aganist the resident priest Sumangala.

Shortsighted Buddhists not knowning the history of the holy shrine sided with the saivite mahant, and the Japanese came to form an alliance with the saivite Mahant to create a political centre at Buddha-gaya.

and the Ceylon Buddhists who are under British Rule were expelled from their holy Shrine in 1910.

The Saivite mahants came into possession of the land at Taradi in the 18th century, but the holy temple which was in ruins was on the zamindari of the Tikari Raj, and the land was known as the Maha Bodhi. For seventeen hundred years the holy shrine was in Buddhist hands. The Prince Siddhartha became Buddha at the Bodhimanda 2506 years ago ; in 1202 A. C. Bakhtiyar Khilji destroyed the holy shrine. About two hundred years ago the saivite mahants occupied the village and neglected the Temple, then in ruins. In March 1833 the Burmese Embassy accompanied by Captain Burney visited Buddha-gaya. Forty years previous to the advent of the Burmese Embassy the mahants erected the baradari on the ground at Taradi not on temple grounds. Since 1833 Burmese Buddhists have been visiting Buddha-gaya. The Buddhists of Ceylon, Burma being subjects of the British Sovereign should ask the Government of His Majesty to place the holy temple and the Bodhi Tree under Buddhist monks. The associations of 1700 years cannot be forgotten. The saivite mahants have no religious interests at the shrine. The worship now being conducted therein by the menials of the mahants was declared as "spurious worship" by the

High Court of Calcutta. The rights of the landlord should be considered and the Buddhists should compensate the mahants most liberally, and the holy Shrine placed under Buddhist custody. The Japanese Buddhists may move in the matter, now that the Japanese are the allies of the British People.

Mecca is in Moslem hands, and with British victory in Palestine Jerusalem will go under Christian jurisdiction ; there is already a movement to establish again the Zion movement at Jerusalem ; Benares is under the Saivite priests ; Gaya Vishnupad is under Vishnu priests ; Brindavan the birthplace of Sree Krishna is also under the Vaishnava priests, only the place of the Buddha's Enlightenment is under non-Buddhist hands. Should the Buddhiats not feel for the hallowed Shrine with seventeen hundred years of sacred associations with the same feeling as the Jews show to Jerusalem and the Moslems to Mecca. The Moslems of Java and Chittagong daily remember Mecca five times in their prayers.

The holy site at Bodhimanda is sacred to the Buddhists from eternity to eternity. It is at Buddha-gaya that the Bodisatvas of the past, present and the future attain to Bnddhahood. The earth is a halting place for the non-Buddhist, but to the Buddhist who believes in the dectrine of rebirth, the earth is the home till Arhatship is gained, and India is the sacred land for all time to come.

For nearly twenty years the Buddhists have failed to respond to the appeals of the Maha Bodhi Society. The present generation has forgotten Buddha-gaya, the past generation of Buddhists of Ceylon and Burma liberally contributed. If the Buddhists of Japan, China, Siam, Burma, and Ceylon love their religion as the Christians love theirs, and the Moslems love Islam, there is every hope that help will be forth coming to spread the holy Doctrine of the Lord Buddha. If the Buddhists really appreciate the sublime teachings of the Tathāgata they will not hesitate to give their support to a movement which is working to revive the holy religion in the land of its birth. In India there are nearly 200 millions of people who need a religion of compassion. The instincts of the Aryan people revolt at animal sacrifices ; Christianity and Islam are alien to the people in spirit ; Brahmanism is only for the high castes ; and the only religion that can help the teeming millions of India is the religion of Compassion of the Buddha, the Aryan prince of the solar line of Ikshvaku.

THE ARYA DHARMA AND THE COMING OF THE BUDDHA OF LOVE

The present kalpa is called the great good kalpa, inasmuch as four Buddhas had already appeared, and the fifth is expected when the new race appears. The present race will continue to deteriorate, righteousness will gradually disappear : injustice, deviation from the path of truth, covetousness, unnatural lust, cruelty will continue to increase. The Kaliyuga according to the Purānas will last for another 250,000 years, and then will begin the dawn of the new manvantara. But according to Buddhist eschatalogy the present race will gradually decline and the race destroyed by various cataclysms, and the remnants of the race will be the nucleus of the new race that will be reborn.

Those that are now walking in the path of righteousness showing mercy to all, abstaining from hurting others , from stealing, from committing adultery, from falsehood, from drinking intoxicating drinks, from following the vicious methods of false teachers, will after death be reborn in the Tusita heaven where the future Buddha is now living

The next Buddha will be born in the Brahman

caste, and the city of his birth will be Benares, which will then be called Ketumati. The age of the people who are born then will be very long, and only righteousness will reign. There will be no killing, stealing and committing adultery, no untruth, no drinking of liquor, no nakedness, no poverty, no mud houses, no filth, no dirt, the cities will be all lighted, and parks, and gardens abound. It will be a heaven on earth.

Those who are now doing good work, and showing kindness to parents, to elders, and to holy men and good Brahmans, and abstain from killing animals, who do not follow heretical doctrines who do not follow the path of naked ascetics, who do not rub ash on their bodies, who give charity to the poor, who follow the doctrine of karma, and who accept the doctrine of rebirth will after death be reborn in the Tusita heaven.

When the new earth and the new race are born the Buddha Maittreyya, the Lord of Love will be reborn in Benares. Those who are now doing good works with faith in the Buddha and those who had already been dead after having done good work ; their place is Tusita. All good Buddhists who had failed to enter one of the four paths of holiness under the Dispensation of the Gautama Buddha will become the disciples of the Lord of Love. For another two thousand and five hundred years the message of the coming Lord will be heard. The yellow robed Bhikkhus will continue to announce the message of deliverance.

The Buddha Gautama in the sermon that He delivered to Bhikkhus called the Cakkavatti sutta, Majjhima nikāya, proclaimed the coming of the great Lord of Love.

Every Buddha teaches the following principles of the Arya Dhamma. The righteous king, the great universal emperor, Rājā Chakravarti, rules his empire by the power of righteousness. He is the first to proclaim the ten daily rules for the observance of his people viz., to abstain from cruelty and destruction of life, from stealing, from committing adultery, from falsehood, foul speech, slander, and intoxicating drinks and drugs, illwill, covetousness and unbelief. The righteous emperor doth see that every one in his empire is not burdened with poverty ; he provides the poor with means, and sees that they are able to gain their livelihood by honest labour and industrial pursuits ; he exhorts people that they should take care of their parents and elders in the family and honour and entertain holy Brahmans and holy Sramanas.

When a perfect all-enlightened Buddha appears, and no two Buddhas appear at the same time, He teaches the five Chakravarti rules for daily observance, and also ten meritorious deeds, viz., Charity, to observe the rules of moral conduct, to practise the development of good thoughts, to honour and to attend to the comforts of parents and teachers and nurse them when they are sick, to show hospitality to strangers, to ask others to share in the good work that one is doing, to accept the share in the good work that others are doing, to preach the Good Law, and to hear the Good Law, and to keep one's faith upright.

On the full-moon days of each month the householder is expected to observe the rules of Brahmachāri life in abstaining from sexual intercourse, from eating at unseasonable hours, and going to places of immoral amusements and dancing parties. On that day he has to abstain from all kinds of luxurious seats, clothes, scents, perfumes etc.

The three paths to Nirvāna are : sammmāsambodhi, pratyeka bodhi, and srāvaka bodhi. The first is the supreme, the second is middling, and the third is low. The Mahāyana path is the path of the supreme bodhisatvas who aspire to become Buddhas, the Majjhima or Ekayāna path is for the pratyeka Buddhas, and the Hinayāna path is for those who wish to enter

Nirvāna quicker without concerning about the salvation
of others. The Hinayāna Bodhisatvas follow a perfect
Buddha, inasmuch as they are unable to discover the
Four Truths by their own efforts. The Pratyeka
Bodhisatvas do not want the help of a perfect
Buddha, and they discover the path, but they are
unable to proclaim the Truths to others. The
Pratyeka Buddhas invariably appear when no fully
enlightened Buddhas appear. The Hinayāna srāvaka
bodhisatvas are born only when an all-enlightened
Buddha appears. They becomes Arahants and
attain Nirvāna on this earth. To attain arhatship
the ten pāramitās have to be practised for one
asankheyya kalpa ; to become a pratyeka Buddha for
two asankheyya kalpas ; to become an all enlightened
Buddha for four asankheyya and one hundred
thousand kalpss. The ten pāramitas are Charity
absolute and universal ; Moral conduct in perfection ;
Renunciation of sensual pleasures and aspiring to
holiness ; Observing the path of Wisdom supreme ;
Strenuous Exertion to reach the goal ; unfaltering
Truthfulness ; Forgiving patience ; Indomitable Will
to reach the Consummation ; Universal love to all
living creatures ; Indifference to praise and blame in
the performance of duty.

214

THE PRINCIPAL DOCTRINES OF THE DHARMA

THE FOUR SATIPATTHANAS : THOUGHT FIXITIES.

Analysis of the Breath and the 32 Categories of the Body.

Analysis of Sense Feelings.

Analysis of ideations (chittas).

Analysis of the five psychical hindrances and of the seven principles of Enlightenment (bojjhangas).

THE FOUR SAMYAK PRADHANA ; RIGHT EXERTIONS.

Exertion to destroy evil thoughts already arisen.

Exertion to prevent Evil thoughts arising.

Exertion to originate meritorious thoughts.

Exertion to develop and increase meritorious thoughts already arisen.

THE FOUR IDDHIPADAS ; BASES OF WORKING WONDERS.

Intense desire to acquire psychical powers and Nirvāna.

The strenuous energy to acquire good karma for the development of psychical powers.

215

Development of meritorious thoughts.

Investigation and analysis of the methods adopted.

THE FIVE INDRIYAS ; SEATS OF POWER.

Faith, Power of Recollection, Strenuous Energy, Psychical Concentration, and Wisdom supreme.

THE FIVE BALA : PSYCHICAL POWERS.

Power of Faith, Power of Recollection, Power of Energy, Power of Psychical Concentration. Power of Supernal Wisdom,

THE SEVEN CONSTITUENTS OF PERFECT ENLIGHTENMENT : BOJJHANGAS,

1. Recollection of the four Contents relating to the formation of the body, sense feelings, ideations, and psychical hindrances and helps,

2. Investigation of the psychical categories of the four noble truths, the thought fixities, indriyas, balas, bojjhangas,

3 Undaunted energy, strenuous exertion to reach the goal.

4. Cheerfulness without hilarity.

5. Serenity and Composure of body.
6. Concentration of meritorious thoughts.
7. Equalmindedness, indifference to praise and blame,

THE NOBLE EIGHTFOLD PATH : ARIYA MAGGANGANI.

1. Right views opposed to nihilistic and unscientific views.
2. Right desires of mercy, loviug kindness, and renunciation of sense pleasures.
3. Right Speech., truthfulness, abstaining from slander, harsh speech, and idle talk.
4. Right Actions-abstinence from destruction of life, stealing, committing adultery and sexual indulgence, and drinking intoxicants.
5. Right Livelihood abstaining from the five sinful professions of slave dealing, selling poisons, intoxicants of kinds, flesh of animals, and murderous weapons.
6. Right Exertion. Exertion to destroy evil thoughts already arisen, Exertion to prevent evil thoughts arising, Exertion to originate meritorious thoughts, Exertion to expand, develop and increase meritorious thoughts already arisen.

7. Right Mindfulness : to analyse the inhalations and exhalations of one's breath, and to analyse the 32 components of the body ; to analyse the differentiating sense feelings ; to analyes the manifold arisings of the heart ; to analyse the five psychical hindrances, and the seven principles of enlightment.

8. Right Psychical Illuminations. The practise of the first, second, third and fourth dhyānas to realize Nirvāna.

THE FIVE PSYCHICAL HINDRANCES : NIVARANAS.

Desire for sexual enjoyment ; Ill-will, hatred, anger ; Sleepiness, Laziness ; Mindwanderings, restlessness ; Scepticism based on nihilism.

THE TWELVE NIDANAS : BASIC ELEMENTS OPERATING INTERDEPENDENTLY CAUSING REBIRTH.

1. Ignorance (Avidya) of the 24 Laws of Cause and Effect.
2. Thought Ideations producing karma (Sankhāras).
3, Cognitions depending on ideations (viññā*n*a).
4, Mind activities and correlative formation of the physical body (nāmarupa).
5. Activities of the six sense organs (salāyatana).

6. Contact produced by activities of the Consciousness depending on objective phenomena with the six sense organs (Phasso).

7. Feelings produced by the sixfold Contact (Vedanā)

8. The Intense Craving for sexual and sensual pleasures of the material and heavenly planes (Tanhā).

9. Psychological Bases of Rebirth which are foolish ascetic habits, retention of the erroneous idea of a permanent ego, desire for sense pleasures in a heavenly form, holding erroneous beliefs (Upādāna.)

10. Re-birth (Realms of Existences) in the kāma, Rupa, and Arupa lokas (Bhavo).

11. The Coming together of the five Skhandhas resulting in individualized rebirth (Jāti).

12. Decay, Dissolution of the body called death, Grief, lamentation, despair, jarā, marana, soka, parideva dukkha, domanassa, upāyāsa).

THE TWELVE NIDANAS CLASSIFIED INTO SEVEN CATEGORICAL GROUPS

First Group : Consists of Nidānas of Ignorance, Ideations, Cravings, Bases of Rebirth, Rebirth

Realms. These nidānas operating in the past life produced karma, which resulted in co-ordination of the nidānas of the present rebirth which may be called the

Second Group : consisting of the nidānas of prati-sandhi Viññāna, rebirth consciousness, mind-and body, six sense organs, Contact and Feelings. The nidānas of the second group forming an individuality produce karma in this present life, form the

Third Group : consisting of the nidānas : Ignorance, Ideations, Cravings, Bases of Rebirth and Realms of Rebirth. These nidānas operating produce karma for rebirth in the next life, and their co-ordination go to form the

Fourth Group : consisting of the nidānas Conception Consciousness, Mind-and-body, Six sense organs, Contact and Feelings.

Fifth Group : consists of nidānas : Ideations and Rebirth Realms of Existences. Ideations produce karma, and karma produce rebirth

Sixth Group : Ignorance, Cravings, Bases of Rebirth, co-ordinating form the field of Contamina tions.

Seventh Group : Consciousness, Mind-and-body, Six

sense organs, Contact, Feelings, are the results of Group Fifth.

FIVE SKHANDHAS.

Body formed of the four changing bhutas, hardness, wateriness, windiness, and heat-called rupa.

Sense Feelings called Vedanā.

Sense Perceptions called Saññā.

Ideations or Karma thoughts called Samkhāras.

Cognitions called Viññāna.

THE TEN FETTERS : SANYOJANAS.

1. Erroneous ideas of a permanent ego inside the body-sakkāya ditthi.

2. Doubt regarding past, and future worlds, and abont the Buddha and Dharma, and unbelief in the law of karma-Vicikicchā.

3. Mortifying asceticism in order to gain heavenly reward-silabbata parāmāsa.

4. Desire for sensual enjoyment in the celestial regions—Kamarāga.

5. Anger, ill-will, hatred—Patigha.

6. Desire to be born in the world of Brahmā and to live permanently there— Ruparāga.

221

7. Desire to be born in the spiritual world where
   only the mind exists—Aruparāga.
8. Pride-māna.
9. Vanity-Uddaccha.
10. Ignorance of the great law of Casuality and the
   Four Noble Truths—Avidyā.

THE THREE CHARACTEISTICS : ANITYAM, DUKKHAM, ANATMAN.

1. That all forms, sensations, perceptions, ideations,
   cognitions, subjective and objective, far
   and near, small and great, invisible and
   visible, are undergoing change momentarily. This is anityam.
2. That which is subject to change can only produce
   sorrow, misery, grief, This is dukkha.
3. That which is subject to change, and productive
   of sorrow is it wise to say "this is mine",
   "this is I", and "I am that" ? This is
   Anātman.

THE THREE CAUSES THAT PRODUCE DEMERITORIOUS KARMA.

1. Covetousness, desire for lustful enjoyment.
2. Anger, hatred, ill-will.

3. Muddleheadedness, Ignorance.

The three causes productive of meritorious Karma (1) Non-covetousness (2) Love, kindness, non-anger (3) Wisdom.

THE SEVEN (VISUDDHI) PURITIES.

1. The purity in Ethical Conduct.
2. The purity in heart.
3. The purity in religious belief.
4. The purity in having all doubts removed about a future life.
5. The purity in wisdom in knowing the true path and the untrue path.
6. The purity in the knowledge of epistemological science.
7. The purity in the science of wisdom.

THE SEVEN STEPS IN THE SCIENCE OF EPISTEMOLOGY.

1. The science of evolution and dissolution.
2. The science of atomic disintegration.
3. The science of knowing the causes of disintegration.
4. The science of realising the fruits of analysis.
5. The science of knowing that freedom is coming.

6. The science of escaping.
7. The science of thoughtful analysis.
8. The science of analysis of sankhāras.
9. The realization of the Noble Truth.

WESTERN INTERPRETERS OF THE DOCTRINE OF THE BUDDHA

The first Western scholar to interpret the religion of the Blessed One to the people of Europe was the Frenchman, Eugene Burnouf. The first European to collect Buddhist texts was Brian Houghton Hodgson, British Resident at the Court of Kathmandu. The first scholar to learn Chinese to translate the life of the great Chinese Buddhist pilgrim Hwen Tsang was Stanislaus Julien, a Frenchman. The first European to learn Tibetan to translate Buddhist works was Csoma d' Korosi. The first European to learn Pāli to translate Buddhist works was George Turnour, the Government Agent, at Kandy, Ceylon. The first English missionary to learn Sinhalese was Spence Hardy.

The names of the European scholars who had helped to translate Buddhist literature into Europeon languages are herein given :—Westergaard, Fausboll, Oldenburg, Spence Hardy, Schiefner, Trenckner Schlaganweit, Stanislaus Julien, Csoma d' Korosi, Dr. Rhys Davids, R. Pischel, E. Senart, Abel Remusat, Barthelemy St. Hilaire, Eugene Burnouf, Brian H.

Hodgson, Cecil Bendall, Serge d' Oldenberg, Prof.
Minayeff, Mrs. Rhys Davids, Dr. Wenzel, Prof.
Windisch, M. Chavennes, Dr. Neumann, Dr. C. R.
Lanman, C. H. Warren, Prof, Hopkins, A. Foucher,
E. Hubers, Victor Henri, Dr. Bloomfield, Otto
Schrader, the German Bhikkhu Nyānatiloka, the
Scotch Bhikkhu Silāchāra, C. T. Strauss, Dr.
Zimmermann, Thomas Hardy, S. Beal, Lavallee
Poussin, Edkins, Otto Franke, Dr. Anderson, Ed
Foucaux, Sylvan Levi, Mrs. Mabel Bode, A. Barth,
Robert Chalmers, B. H. T. Francis, E. Cowell, E. J.
Thomas, Dr. Rouse, Norman, Richard Morris, Estlin
Carpenter, R. C. Childers, Edwin Arnold, R. F.
Johnston, Monier Williams, Johnson, H. S. Olcott,
Dr. Paul Carus, Timothy Richard, Gogerly, Dr. Eitel,
Lafcadio Hearn, Max Muller, Alabaster, A. Weber,
H. Kern, F. L. Woodward and H. P. Blavatsky.

Buddhist workers in India to-day are, the
Anagārika Dharmapāla, pioneer of Indian Buddhist
Revival, Kiripā Mahathero, leader of Chittagong
Buddhists, Samana Punnānanda, Charu Chandra
Bose, Dr. Satis Chandra Vidyabhusana. Prof.
Lakshmi Narasu, M. Singaravelu Chetty, Pandit
Kosambi Dharmānanda, Dr. Beni Madav Barua,
Chandramani Bhikkhu, Mahavir Thero and Rai Saheb
Isan Chandra Ghose.

Ciram ti*tt*hatu saddammo

Dhamme hontu sagāravā

Sabbepi sadākālena

Sammā devo pavassatu

Sammā vassatu kālena

Devopi jagati pati

Saddhamma nirato lokam

Dhammen eva pasāsatu

Ciram ti*tt*hatu lokasmim

Sammā sambuddha sāsanam

Tasmim sagāravā niccam

Hontu sabbepi pānino."

Commentary.

APPENDIX

No. 154.

GOVERNMENT OF INDIA

DEPARTMENT OF EDUCATION.

(Archy).

Simla, the 30th June, 1916.

FROM

THE HON'BLE SIR E. D. MACLAGAN, K.C.I.E., C.S.I.,

Secretary to the Government of India

To

THE SECRETARY OF THE GOVERNMENT

OF BENGAL

General Department.

SIR,

I am directed to state for the information of the Governor in Council that several Buddhist Relics have recently been found in various stupas at Taxila in the Rawal-pindi District of the Punjab dating from about the beginning of the Christian era. The Government of India are advised though it cannot be affirmed that they were relics of the Buddha himself, they were undoubtedly regarded with veneration two thousand years ago.

2. In addition to the above there is a well authenticated relic of the Buddha consisting of small piece of bone contained in a rock crystal casket which was discovered in 1892 at Bhattiprolu in the Kristna district of the Madras Presidency. This relic is now in the Government Central Museum, Madras. An account of its discovery appears on pages 11-12 of volume XV. of the new Imperial series of Reports of the Archaeological Survey of India and a translation of the inscription engraved on the relic box is given in a list of Brahmi inscriptions prepared by Professor Luders *vide* pages 158—159 of volume X. of the Epigraphia Indica. The date of these inscriptions which are in the early Brahmi script is the second century B. C.

3. I am to say that the Government of India will be prepared to present three of the relics including the Bhattiprolu relic to the Maha-Bodhi Society, (4-A, College Square, Calcutta) and one to the Bengal Buddhist Association, (5, Lalit Mohan Das Lane, Kapalitola, Calcutta), provided that both Societies can guarantee that the relics will be enshrined in worthy *Viharas* and adequately safe-guarded and provided that the shrines are constructed before the relics are distributed.

4. I am to request that, with the permission of

the Governor in Council, that the Societies may be informed accordingly. I am also to ask that it may be suggested to the Maha-Bodhi Society that they should enshrine the three relics at Calcutta, Sarnath and Taxila, respectively.

I have &c.,

(Sd.) E. D. MACLAGAN,

Secretary to the Govt. of India.

No. 1022.

GOVERNMENT OF BENGAL

GENERAL DEPARTMENT

Miscellaneous Branch.

Calcutta, the 31st July 1916.

FROM

C. W. GURNER, Esq., I. C. S.,

Under-Secretary to the Government of Bengal.

To

THE SECRETARY TO THE MAHA-BODHI SOCIETY,

4-A, College Square, Calcutta.

Sir,

I am directed to forward a copy of the marginally

noted letter from the Government of India, Department of Education and to inquire
whether the Maha-Bodhi Society is
desirous of accepting the relics on the
conditions laid down. If so, I am to request that you
will report at an early date what arrangements the
Society proposes to make for enshrining and safe-
guarding them in a suitable manner at Calcutta,
Sarnath and Taxila.

No. 154, dated
the 30th July.
1916.

I have &c.,

(Sd.) C. W. GURNER.

Under-Secy. to the Govt. India.